Psychology FOR KIDS VOL.1

40 FUN TESTS THAT HELP YOU LEARN ABOUT YOURSELF

Jonni Kincher

free spirit
PUBLISHING®

Library of Congress Cataloging-in-Publication Data

Kincher, J., 1949–

      Psychology for kids vol. 1 (updated) : 40 fun tests that help you learn about yourself /
J. Kincher ; edited by Julie Bach and Pamela Espeland.

           p. cm.

      Includes bibliographical references and index.

      ISBN 978-1-57542-283-1

 1. Character tests—Juvenile literature. 2. Personality tests—Juvenile literature. 3. Self-evaluation—Juvenile literature. 4. Self-report inventories. I. Bach, Julie S. II. Espeland, Pamela. III. Title.

      BF831.K55 2008

      155.2'83—dc22

                                  2008020660

Reading Level Grades 5–6; Interest Level Ages 10 & Up; Fountas & Pinnell Guided Reading Level V

Edited by Julie Bach and Pamela Espeland
Cover and interior design by Tasha Kenyon
Illustrated by Patricia Storms

10 9 8 7 6 5 4 3 2
Printed in the United States of America
V20280710

Free Spirit Publishing Inc.
217 Fifth Avenue North, Suite 200
Minneapolis, MN 55401-1299
(612) 338-2068
help4kids@freespirit.com
www.freespirit.com

Free Spirit Publishing is a member of the Green Press Initiative, and we're committed to printing our books on recycled paper containing a minimum of 30% post-consumer waste (PCW). For every ton of books printed on 30% PCW recycled paper, we save 5.1 trees, 2,100 gallons of water, 114 gallons of oil, 18 pounds of air pollution, 1,230 kilowatt hours of energy, and .9 cubic yards of landfill space. At Free Spirit it's our goal to nurture not only young people, but nature too!

green press INITIATIVE

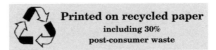

Printed on recycled paper
including 30%
post-consumer waste

DEDICATION

To Beth Jacobs, a shining star who captures the spirit of this book. She is a friend who listens and understands, who helps others know themselves and the world around them. May we all consider her example and continue to pass the tests we give each other daily: tests of patience, kindness, and loyalty. Having passed all of these tests, we will know that our relationships have stood the biggest test of all… the test of time.

ACKNOWLEDGMENTS

To all dedicated teachers-past, present, and future, especially:

- Dr. Patrick Egan, my best teacher; Mr. Ed Pola, an extraordinary volunteer who taught so many so well, including my own children; Linda Price, who has spent a lifetime inspiring brand new readers (authors love that); and Kristina Cilmi Naftzger, a former student who is carrying on the tradition of "deep teaching" to the next generation.

- Adam Kincher gave generously of his time in proofreading and editing help, as well as Web design. Thank you.

- Finally, I want to thank my readers—past, present, and future. May you always find ways to connect what you find on the inside to the greater world outside.

CONTENTS

Your Creative Styles

Your Thinking Styles

Your Learning Styles

Special Styles

FOREWORD

Psychology is the study of human thoughts, feelings, and behaviors. Like any field of study, it has its own special methods and language. These often seem mysterious and complicated to "outsiders," and this makes people suspicious of psychology. They may think, "If others have knowledge about me, then they can control me or use this knowledge against me."

What if we turn this idea around and say, "If I have knowledge about myself, then I have the freedom and the opportunity to control my own life—the freedom to choose my own way"? Knowledge that leads to personal freedom is the theme of *Psychology for Kids Vol. 1.*

This book is about the process of personal exploration, and the reward of personal insight that is available to anyone who wanders within its pages. Aimed primarily at young people ages 10 and up, this book is fun and useful for anyone who wants to learn more about himself or herself.

Author J. Kincher leads us on a creative journey into ourselves. Each page, each Personal Style Inventory reveals new paths. She covers many possibilities and topics along the way, continually stimulating our thoughts and inspiring us to want to know more. She does not direct or control our journey; she believes we should be in charge of where we go and what we discover when we get there. Our discoveries might change us a little or a lot. The ultimate goal is not change, though, but the pure pleasure of finding out about ourselves—who we are, how we are the way we are, why it matters to know.

When we share our knowledge and insights with each other, we begin to appreciate ourselves more. We also begin to appreciate others more. After all, if we're this interesting, then maybe they are, too!

This book puts psychology where it can be of most value: into the hands and minds of young people, whose natural curiosity and willingness to learn make them especially well suited for any journey of self-discovery.

Thomas Elliott, Ph.D.
Clinical Psychologist in Private Practice
Redlands, California

INTRODUCTION

Almost nobody likes to take tests. And that probably includes you. But the tests in this book are different. They're fun to take. In fact, they're so much fun that they're almost like games, except for one big difference: They teach you things about yourself. Important, interesting, helpful things you may be surprised to learn.

The tests in this book have a special name. They're called PSIs—**P**ersonal **S**tyle **I**nventories—because they tell you about your personal style.

When I say "personal style," I don't mean your clothes or the way you wear your hair. In this book, and in other books about psychology, personal style means a person's *attitudes, opinions, beliefs, habits, choices, memories, ideas, feelings,* and *abilities.*

Are you an extrovert or an introvert? An optimist or a pessimist? Are you creative? Are you a genius? Are you right-brained or left-brained? What body language do you speak? Can you predict the future? The answers to these questions are clues to your personal style. This book will help you find your own answers.

Knowing your personal style helps you to know yourself.

> "He who knows others is learned. He who knows himself is wise."
> —*Lao Tse, philosopher*

WHAT'S SO IMPORTANT ABOUT KNOWING YOURSELF?

Many people are a mystery to themselves. They don't understand the things they do, the things they say, or even the things they think. They may be able to tell you a lot about their parents, brothers and sisters, or friends, but when it comes to talking about themselves, they're stumped!

When you know yourself, you can be true to yourself. You can make choices and decisions that are right for you. You can make plans—for today, for tomorrow, for your life—that "fit" who you are. When someone suggests a plan that doesn't fit who you are—like joining a certain club, or preparing for a certain career—you'll know it isn't right for you.

Many people let others tell them what to do and think. Sometimes this means that they go against their own personal style. This can cause problems. What about the doctor who wishes she had been an artist? Or the artist who wishes he had been a plumber? Or the plumber who always yearned to be an astronaut? Or the astronaut who dreams about raising pigs? The point is this: If you spend your life going against your personal style, you probably won't be very happy.

Knowing yourself—knowing your personal style—can help you shape your own future, choose your own direction, make your own decisions, and follow your own dreams.

ABOUT THE PSIs

Many of the PSIs in *Psychology for Kids Vol. 1* are based on tests that experts use. Others have been developed especially for young people. Many young people have already used the PSIs in this book to learn more about themselves. Read what some of them have said:

- "Doing the tests was very interesting. It is always fun to see what kind of person you really are, not just what you *think* you are." —*Kjrste, 14*

- "I know that if I study about myself, I will be able to study almost anybody. I think that it's okay to be different from others."—*Felicity, 11*

- "It's neat to find out things about myself that I never thought about." —*Vinod, 13*

- "It is so important to me, especially as a teenager, to learn the most I can about what's going on inside me. I'm stuck in between being a grown-up and a child and I need all the help "I can get to see what my feelings are all about. The closer I am with myself, the closer I can be to other people." —*Kristina, 15*

PSIs aren't like the tests you take in school. Those tests help you learn about science, math, reading, and other subjects. PSIs help you learn about yourself.

PSIs also aren't like the aptitude tests you may have taken in school. Aptitude tests help you learn about what you can do. PSIs help you learn about what you like to do.

You can use PSIs together with other kinds of tests to make choices and decisions about your life. For example, school tests and aptitude tests may tell you that you're good at math. So maybe you plan a career in computer science. Meanwhile, PSIs may tell you that you enjoy working with large groups of people. So maybe you decide to work for a big company instead of a small one.

Here's another way PSIs are different from tests you take in school: They have absolutely NO control over your life. Nobody is going to make judgments about you based on your PSIs. Nobody is going to say, "You can't take this course, or go to this college, or choose this career," based on your PSIs. Some tests close doors; PSIs can only open doors. They are tools for self-discovery.

The best thing about PSIs is . . . there are no wrong answers! These are tests you just can't fail!

"You are what you are. It is my opinion the trouble in the world comes from people who do not know what they are, and pretend to be something else."

—*Lillian Hellman, playwright*

TIPS FOR TAKING THE PSIs

- Each PSI has its own instructions and its own scoring system. Start by reading the directions carefully.

- Answer the questions as honestly as you can.

- Give the first answer that comes to your mind.

- What if you want to take the PSIs again a few months or years from now? Make this book reusable by writing your responses in pencil. Or photocopy the pages you want to write on. Or print pages from the CD-ROM. Or write your responses on separate sheets of paper, perhaps in a special spiral-bound note-book. (Be sure to write the number of the PSI and the date on each page.)

- You can take the PSIs in order, or skip around. Do them by yourself, or with friends, family, or classmates. Do all of them, or just a few. This book is for you to use any way you like.

- After you take a PSI, think about how your answers might have been different two or three years ago. Think about how they might be different two or three years from now. What does this tell you about your personal style? Does it change? Does it stay the same?

- On pages 119–122, you'll find a Grand Score Sheet. Fill it out when you're finished with all the PSIs (or as many as you want to do). This will give you a big picture of your personal style.

- Don't be worried or afraid if you learn something about yourself that surprises you. If you feel like it, tell an adult you trust and can talk to.

FIVE IMPORTANT THINGS TO REMEMBER ABOUT ALL TESTS, INCLUDING PSIs

1. No test is perfect. All tests are made by humans, and humans make mistakes. Even very official tests like the S.A.T., the A.C.T., or the Iowa Test of Basic Skills contain "questionable" questions.

2. If a test tells you something about yourself that you know isn't true, then the test is probably wrong, not you!

3. The way you feel when you take a test can affect your answers. The best time to take a test is when you're feeling most "like yourself"—not too happy, not too sad, not too excited, not too bored. Try never to take any test when you're feeling sick or very tired.

4. Almost every test will have questions you disagree with or don't like. Don't worry about it. Just answer them in the best way you can.

5. Different people will have different ideas about what test questions mean. Their ideas are valuable. *So are yours.*

Good luck, and have fun learning about yourself!

—Jonni Kincher

A SPECIAL NOTE TO PARENTS AND TEACHERS

The PSIs in *Psychology for Kids Vol.1* are based on psychological theories and research. However, they are not meant to be statistically significant, nor do they purport to follow the validity or reliability standards applied to "official" psychological tests. Those tests take years of research and statistical data for verification. My PSIs have been "field-tested" in real classes with real children, but in no way should they be interpreted as the last word on a particular child's abilities, attitudes, feelings, and beliefs. Their purpose is simple: to stimulate and enhance the process of self-discovery, which is every child's right. They are also designed to be fun. Children should enjoy learning about themselves!

A child who asks for this book or receives it as a gift should be free to do the PSIs whenever he or she chooses, in whatever order he or she prefers. (That's what self-discovery is all about.) Teachers using it in the classroom might find it helpful to schedule specific PSIs around special days or times of the year. Here are some suggestions for working *Psychology for Kids Vol.1* into the curriculum:

- **PSI #40: Can You Predict the Future?** is a good way to start the New Year. So is **PSI #17: Setting Priorities.**

- **PSI #4: Do You Think in Stereotypes?** and **PSI #20: Are You a Leader?** fit well with Dr. Martin Luther King Jr. Day.

- **PSI #28: Are You a Real Genius?** is appropriate for Presidents' Day.

- Try **PSI #36: Are You Superstitious?** with any Friday the 13th.

- Use **PSI #1: Are You an Optimist or a Pessimist?** to start the spring season.

- **PSI #35: Are You a Lone Learner or a Team Player?** complements cooperative learning activities.

- **PSI #32: How Observant Are You?** can introduce Columbus Day.

- **PSI #8: How Many Personas Do You Have?** can be used at Halloween.

- **PSI #15: Mood Food** goes well with the Thanksgiving feasting season.

- **PSI #14: Mood Music** complements the December holiday season.

In the course of completing the PSIs, some children may discover things that surprise or concern them. In the Introduction, I encourage the young reader to "tell an adult you trust and can talk to." If your child or student comes to you with a question or an issue that stems from a PSI, please take this seriously.

Take a look at the PSI the child is referring to, and ask to see the child's answers. (If the child says no, don't press it.) In any event, talk things over. Reassure the child that there's nothing "wrong" with her or him. Seek advice from other experts, if that seems best.

Suggest that the child read more about the particular question or issue. On page 125 of this book, there's a section called Read More About It that can serve as a starting point for finding appropriate books. The Bibliography on page 126 might lead you to additional useful resources. Guide the child's reading, and always be willing to listen and talk. Often, that's all a child really needs.

PSI #1

ARE YOU AN OPTIMIST OR A PESSIMIST?

The world is full of optimists and pessimists. Optimists tend to look on the bright side of things. They find the good in almost any situation. Pessimists tend to worry about bad things that might happen. They see potential problems in almost any situation. We need both in the world—optimists to give us encouragement, and pessimists to keep us cautious.

PART 1: When you look at these pictures, what do you think of first? Circle A or B for each one.

1

A. half full

B. half empty

2

A. beautiful weaving

B. icky spider web

3

A. an idea

B. danger

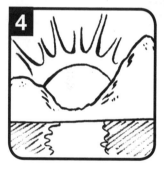

4

A. new day dawns

B. old day dies

5

A. young love

B. graffiti

6

A. future classic

B. used car

7

A. holidays are coming

B. vacation is over

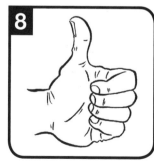

8

A. "thumbs up" sign

B. hitchhiker

PART II

When you read these words, what do you think of first?
Circle **A** or **B** for each one.

1. ROCKY ROAD
A. ice cream
B. tough time

2. FUDGE
A. candy
B. cheat

3. FALL
A. beautiful season
B. tumble

4. FLIGHT
A. upward journey
B. running away

5. SNAP
A. easy
B. break

6. TRICK
A. magic
B. to deceive

7. STROKE
A. to pet
B. a physical ailment

8. TRIP
A. vacation
B. stumble

WHAT'S YOUR STYLE?

TOTAL YOUR A'S AND B'S FROM PARTS I AND II.

A'S	B'S

- 10 or more A's mean you may be an optimist.
- 10 or more B's mean you may be a pessimist.

REMEMBER, WE NEED BOTH IN THE WORLD!

Find Out MORE

✷ Give each member of your family this PSI, then share scores. Are you a family of optimists or pessimists?

✷ Did you get a high score in either category? Try being the opposite for a day. How does it feel?

"The man who is a pessimist before 48 knows too much; if he is an optimist after it, he knows too little." —Mark Twain, humorist

THE OPTIMIST AND THE PESSIMIST: A FABLE

By Randy Flood
When he wrote this story, Randy Flood was a junior at North Bend High School in North Bend, Oregon, and one of the best debaters on the debate team.

A long time ago in a land that was not too far from here, there was a king who had two sons. One son, Adam, was an incurable optimist. The other son, Argot, was a pessimist. Adam and Argot were twins, and there was great debate in the kingdom over which son should take the throne when the king died. Before he died, the king decided that the council of his closest advisers would make the decision.

After the king died, the council decided that Adam and Argot should walk through the kingdom and have a debate over whether it was good or bad. The brother who won the debate was to be king. And so it came to pass that Adam, Argot, and the council walked through the kingdom.

As they walked, they came upon some starving peasants. "Look," Argot said, "they have no food and they are starving. Surely this is proof that the world is a terrible place."

"No," Adam replied, "for lack of sustenance refines the soul. They may have no food, but they are learning a great lesson. Patience is more valuable than food."

Walking a little farther, they came upon a blind man. "Surely the world is a terrible place, when God allows men to go blind!" Argot said.

"Again you are wrong," Adam replied. "Though this man cannot see, his other senses have grown stronger. He can tell if men are lying by the sound of their voices. He is better off blind."

Finally they came upon a sick man who was about to die. "This is terrible!" Argot exclaimed. "A man dies by the side of the road, and no one cares enough to help him. This is proof that the world is a terrible place."

"All men die," Adam answered. "It is not a bad thing to die. This man will soon be with God."

"I have heard enough," said one of the council members. "It is obvious to me who would make a better ruler. Adam showed that the starving peasants were learning the lesson of patience. He showed that the blind man had superior senses, and that the dying man was better off dead. What can Argot possibly say now?"

"Permit me, if you will, to give a small demonstration," Argot said. "Is the primary goal of the ruler to help the people?"

"Yes, of course," the council agreed.

"How can a ruler help the people if he cannot see their problems?" Argot asked.

"I would be able to see their problems, if they had any," Adam said. "But I assure you that they don't."

"You believe that the blind man was better off blind?" Argot asked them all.

"Yes," they answered together.

"Then close your eyes," Argot instructed. "All of you, close your eyes. Now, do you believe that patience is better than food?"

"Yes," they answered again, their eyes tightly closed.

"Then I ask that no one open their eyes until I command it," Argot said.

Silently, Argot drew his sword and slew his brother. He then cleaned his sword and put it away. "Open your eyes now," he said.

"Oh, my God," they cried, "Adam is dead! You have killed your own brother!"

"Then your decision should be an easy one," Argot replied.

"But we would have chosen Adam!" one of the council members said.

"I have won the debate," Argot explained. "Being blind prevented you from stopping me from murdering my brother. Thus, being blind is not so good. Being patient kept you from opening your eyes and seeing what I was doing. Thus, being patient is not so good. And if people are better off dead, then my brother is better off dead, and what I did is justified. Adam is dead, and so you must proclaim me King."

"Well spoken, Argot," the highest council member said. Then he turned to the others. "I believe that Argot is the new king."

All the council agreed, and so it was that Argot the Great ascended to the throne. He ruled for many years, and though he was unhappy most of the time, the land and the people prospered.

TIME OUT: HOW TO MAKE UP YOUR OWN PERSONALITY TESTS

Personality tests are fun to take. They're also fun to make up and try out on other people. You can make up your own personality tests. Here's an idea to get you started.

OPTIMIST/PESSIMIST TEST

1. Make a list of heteronyms. Heteronyms are words that have two meanings and two pronunciations. Some examples are:

PRESENTS
PRE-sents = gifts

pre-SENTS = gives to

OBJECT
OB-ject = an item

ob-JECT = to protest something

INCENSE
IN-cense = a stick or pellet that gives off a fragrant odor when you burn it

in-CENSE = to make angry

CONTRACT
CON-tract = a formal agreement

con-TRACT = to shrink

2. Use your list of heteronyms to make up your own optimist/pessimist test. You can model your test on Part I or Part II of PSI #1.

3. Figure out a way to score your test.

4. Make copies of your test.

5. Have your friends take your test.

6. Afterward, check your test for validity.

In test-making language, "validity" means that a test actually measures what it's supposed to measure. For example, the S.A.T. for college admission is supposed to be a valid test. If it is, then students who do well on the S.A.T. should also do well in college.

You can use this question to check your Optimist/Pessimist Test for validity: "Do the people who scored high in optimism seem like optimistic people?" What other questions can you think of?

You can make up other tests and test questions based on your own ideas, or on other ideas you find in this book. Making up your own tests should give you insight into how test-makers think—and help you when you study for your next school or aptitude test.

PSI #2

ARE YOU AN INTROVERT OR AN EXTROVERT?

You probably know people who are outgoing, and people who are shy. Psychologists have names for each type of person. They call outgoing people *extroverts.*

They call people who are quiet and prefer small groups *introverts.* Which is it better to be, an extrovert or an introvert? Neither! The world needs both kinds of people. And it needs people who fall everywhere in between.

Read these pairs of statements. Which one sounds most like you? Circle A or B for each one

1
A. I am not easily bored.
B. I am easily bored.

2
A. I don't like fast, scary rides.
B. I love being scared by fast rides.

3
A. I would rather spend the evening at home quietly with a few friends.
B. I would rather spend the evening at a loud party with lots of people.

4
A. I enjoy being alone at times.
B. I hate to be alone.

5
A. I like to have a few close friends.
B. I like to have many casual friends.

6
A. I would rather write a book than sell things to people.
B. I would rather sell things to people than write a book.

7
A. I'm not likely to take a dare.
B. I'll take almost any dare.

8
A. I think April Fools' Day is stupid.
B. I think April Fools' Day is really fun.

9
A. You won't find me watching "The Three Stooges."
B. I think "The Three Stooges" are really funny.

10
A. I enjoy talking about ideas.
B. I would rather do things than discuss them.

11
A. In hide-and-seek, you'll find me behind the tree.
B. In hide-and-seek, you'll find me in the tree.

12
A. I avoid crowds.
B. I like crowds.

13
A. I don't like to dance.
B. I like to dance.

14
A. Convertibles aren't safe; you shouldn't ride in one.
B. Convertibles are fun; you should ride in one.

15
A. I enjoy working behind-the-scenes.
B. I want to be on stage.

WHAT'S YOUR STYLE?
TOTAL YOUR A'S AND B'S.

A'S	B'S

- 10 or more A's mean you may be an introvert. You're more comfortable when you're not in social situations. You may feel that other people draw energy from you.

- 10 or more B's mean you may be an extrovert. You're happiest when you're with other people. You may feel that you draw energy from being around them.

- If you got about the same number of A's and B's, you probably feel comfortable wherever you are, with people or alone.

Find Out MORE

✶ Give this PSI to the members of your family, then share scores. Are they extroverts or introverts?

✶ If you're an extrovert, plan some introverted activities to enjoy.

✶ If you're an introvert, plan some extroverted activities to enjoy.

SHOULD YOU CHANGE YOUR STYLE?

Some introverts think they're too shy and wish they could be different. But there's nothing wrong with being quiet, enjoying solitude, or thinking a lot. If you really believe you're too introverted, tell an adult you trust and can talk to.

Some extroverts are very funny people. But after a while, they can get tired of being the life of the party. If you're an extrovert and you get tired, take a break. Let your family and friends know that you'd like to stop being funny for a while.

What if you're an introvert, and you suddenly feel like being in a crowd? Or you're an extrovert, and you get the urge to spend a day alone in your room? Does this mean your personality is changing? Of course not! Sometimes introverts feel like extroverts, and sometimes extroverts feel like introverts. You don't have to be the same all the time. What's important is to be yourself.

CHOOSE YOUR SUPERPOWERS

Have you ever wished you could fly? Or maybe you've wished you could be invisible. It would be wonderful to have such superpowers! Even if you can't have real superpowers, the kinds you wish for can tell you something about yourself. Your wishes may even give you insight into a job or career you'd be good at someday.

Read this list of superpowers and check the two you'd most like to have.

☐ The power to change forms (to look like other people or things)

☐ The ability to hear things clearly over great distances

☐ Time-travel ability

☐ The ability to fly

☐ Invisibility

☐ X-ray vision

☐ The ability to see into the future

☐ The ability to read minds

WHAT'S YOUR STYLE?

IF YOU CHOSE THE POWER TO CHANGE FORMS . . .

You may be a sociable person who likes to "fit in." Perhaps you want to be admired by the group. Maybe you're a real crowd-pleaser!

CAREER CLUES: Entertainment might be the field for you. Actors can "change forms" and be other people.

IF YOU CHOSE "SUPER HEARING" . . .

You probably pay close attention to sounds and patterns. You may like to be fully informed about the latest news. Maybe you're even nosy!

CAREER CLUES: You might make an excellent reporter or gossip columnist. Or you might decide to become a musician.

IF YOU CHOSE TIME TRAVEL . . .

You may be interested in the causes of things and how past mistakes can be used to shape the future. You're probably very curious about how different people live.

CAREER CLUES: A career in scientific research, history, or human behavior might be the place for you. You might enjoy a job where you can affect the future.

IF YOU CHOSE FLYING . . .

Perhaps you like to see the "big picture" of life and how things fit together. Little details may annoy you. You probably enjoy being free and taking risks.

CAREER CLUES: You'd probably make a good pilot or astronaut. Or consider working with big, sweeping ideas that will make a difference in the world. Look for a job that will let you affect policies, maybe in government or a public research group. Avoid getting tied down.

"On a windy day
let's go flying
There may be no trees
to rest on
There may be no clouds
to ride
But we'll have our wings
and the wind will be
with us
That's enough for me,
that's enough for me."

—Yoko Ono, artist and writer, "Song for John"

IF YOU CHOSE INVISIBILITY . . .

You may be shy, or you may be a very keen observer. Or you may be both. Perhaps you like to know everything that is going on around you.

CAREER CLUES: Some good careers for observers are writer, artist, or private investigator. (Remember: Encyclopedia Brown started young!)

IF YOU CHOSE X-RAY VISION . . .

Perhaps you like to "see through" problems and go to the heart of an issue. You might enjoy finding problems that other people can't even see. You also might enjoy solving problems.

CAREER CLUES: Physics, politics, math, and medicine are fields that need skilled problem-solvers.

IF YOU CHOSE SEEING INTO THE FUTURE . . .

You're probably very creative and love adventure. You'd move right into the future if you could! Perhaps you're always looking at what might be possible, and wondering how to make it happen sooner.

CAREER CLUES: A career on the cutting edge of things might be right for you. Think about becoming an explorer, research scientist, inventor, or science fiction writer.

IF YOU CHOSE MIND READING . . .

You're probably good at guessing what other people think. Perhaps you can "see behind" what they're saying to what they're really thinking.

CAREER CLUES: You might be a good counselor or psychologist. It's important for professionals in those careers to understand how other people think and feel.

Find Out MORE

✴ Write a story about yourself. In the story, give yourself the two super-powers you chose. What would you do? Where would you go? What, if anything, would you change about the world?

✴ Ask a friend to choose two super-powers. Spend an afternoon together pretending you have those powers. Can you use your special powers to help each other? Try writing a skit and performing it for your family or classmates.

MORE THAN MAKE-BELIEVE

Everything you're interested in, every choice you make, tells you something about yourself. But you have to think about your choices to understand what they mean.

The special powers listed in this PSI can be more than make-believe. You can be invisible by being quiet and listening. You can read other people's minds by listening and being compassionate. You can fly by going beyond your expectations.

What are other ways you can make these superpowers come true for you?

PSI #4

DO YOU THINK IN STEREOTYPES?

A *stereotype* is an idea about a thing or a group that may be untrue or only partly true. It's a judgment based on one or two pieces of information that don't tell the whole story. Stereotypes often are shared by many people. Some examples of popular stereotypes are: "Smart people aren't athletic." "Rich people are snobs." "Politicians are dishonest." The truth is: Some smart people are very athletic. Many rich people aren't snobs at all. And there really are some honest politicians!

PART I: Describe the four people listed below. Tell how they dress, what kinds of cars they drive, what pets they own, what their hobbies are, and anything else you can think of.

1. A Snob
2. A Genius
3. A Rock Star
4. A Used-Car Salesperson

Tell or read your descriptions to a family member or friend. See if he or she can guess which person you are describing.

PART II: The four students named below turned in identical homework assignments. But two got A's, and two got B's. Which ones received which grades?

Student	Grade
David	
Hubert	
Bertha	
Karen	

Read this question to a family member or friend. Ask her or him to guess the answer. Compare your guesses.

PART III: Circle one word in each pair of words.

1. Joey is (younger/older) than Joe and also somewhat (tougher/cuter).
2. Robert is more (easy-going/particular) than Bob, and Bob seems a little (older/younger) than Robbie.
3. Michael is a lot (more/less) fun to be around than Mike. Mickey is (worse/better) at baseball than either Michael or Mike.
4. Jeanette is (more/less) sophisticated than Jan. Jan is (harder/easier) to get to know.
5. Patricia is (better/worse) at math than Trish.
6. Mandy is (older/younger) than Amanda. Amanda has (worse/better) taste.
7. Phillip is (better/worse) at fixing cars than Phil. Phil is (more/less) fun to be with.
8. When your car breaks down in the middle of nowhere, J.B. Barker is (more/less) likely to help you than Jim-Bob Barker.
9. Samantha is (more/less) likely to be the life of the party than Sam.
10. Rebecca is (more/less) likely to get you to the airport on time than Becky.

Invite a family member or friend to do this exercise. Compare your choices.

WHAT'S YOUR STYLE?

What's in a name? A lot, it seems. Based on nothing but first names, you made judgments about people's intelligence, athletic ability, personality, age, looks, and more!

Was it easy or hard for you to make these judgments? If it was easy, then perhaps you think in stereotypes.

You can start to see the problem with stereotypes. They narrow your mind. They keep you from learning the whole story about someone or something. They can keep you from making friends with someone you might really like.

THE GREAT NAME EXCHANGE

Do these famous characters seem different when they trade names? How? Why?

Freddie Chopin——Frederick Prince Jr.

Mike Mouse——Mickey Myers

Al Einstein——Albert Gore

Chris Walken——Christopher Rock

Katie Zeta Jones——Catherine Holmes

Barbra Doll——Barbie Streisand

Matthew Damon——Matt McConaughey

Jimmy Bond——James Fallon

Jenny Aniston——Jennifer McCarthy

Mandy Bynes——Amanda Moore

John Depp——Johnny Stamos

Bill Smith——President Will Clinton

Thomas Cruise——Tom Jefferson

David Matthews——Dave Beckham

Find Out MORE

✻ Have you ever been hurt by a stereotype? Maybe you couldn't join the baseball team because "girls can't play baseball." Maybe you felt embarrassed one day because "boys don't cry." Maybe other people have made judgments about you because of your age, your race, your religion, your family, where you live, or some other reason. Write about this experience. If you feel like it, talk it over with an adult you trust.

✻ Create a "No Stereotypes Allowed!" poster for your classroom or a room in your home. Find or draw pictures that aren't stereotypes.

Can you add to this list? Invite your friends and family to play along.

_____

_____

_____

_____

_____

_____

_____

MORE NAME GAMES

For each question, give the first answer that comes into your head. Then turn the page around to read the real answers.

1. Who is most likely to be a quicker thinker, Chris Anderson or Chris Zymakas?

2. Sam, Mike, and Brad are triplets. They look alike. They act alike. It's almost impossible to tell them apart. Melanie meets all three of them, then falls in love with one of them. Which will Melanie marry?

1. According to a study done by psychologist Stephen Williams, the letter your last name starts with really does make a difference. In many classrooms today, students are still seated in alphabetical order. Those at the top of the alphabet sit in front and are called on more often. They get more practice in quick thinking. Meanwhile, students at the bottom of the alphabet can let their minds wander.

2. Melanie will probably marry Mike, say researchers Richard Kopelman and Dorothy Lang. Alliteration (words or names that start with the same sound or letter) seems to affect which partners people pick. When Kopelman and Lang looked at the names of over 42,000 married couples in the United States, they found more alliteration than they expected—and more than could be explained away by "chance." Can you think of other couples with same-sounding names? What about Donald Duck and Daisy? Mickey Mouse and Minnie?

PSI #5

WHAT ARE YOUR LIMITS?

Nearly everything in the world has a limit. You can drive to San Francisco from New York, but the ocean limits you from driving to Tokyo. You don't jump off a cliff because you know you can't fly. There are other kinds of limits in our lives. They are set by our parents, friends, society, and government. For example, our parents may tell us what time to go to bed at night. Our friends may tell us to act or dress a certain way. Society tells us not to eat soup with our fingers. The government sets speed limits, among other laws.

We also set limits for ourselves. Some of these help us. For example, we decide not to stay up all night watching TV on the day before an important test. Or we limit the amount of sugar we eat.

Some limits keep us from doing things we really want to do. But we can choose to push our limits. Jim Abbott was born without a hand. He didn't let that stop him from becoming a pitcher for the California Angels baseball team.

Read these statements. Mark each one with an A if you agree, a D if you disagree.

_____ 1. Everything worth inventing has already been invented.

_____ 2. Time travel is impossible.

_____ 3. Science has made all of its major breakthroughs.

_____ 4. None of the basic laws of science will ever be proved wrong.

_____ 5. Social problems like hunger and war will always exist.

_____ 6. Humans are destined to repeat the mistakes of history.

_____ 7. No one will ever travel faster than the speed of light.

_____ 8. I could never be a skydiver.

_____ 9. There is less to discover now than there used to be.

_____ 10. People should mind their own business and not try to solve social problems.

WHAT'S YOUR STYLE?

TOTAL YOUR A'S AND D'S.

A'S	D'S

- **6 or more D's may mean that you place few limits on the world (and yourself).**

- **About equal numbers of A's and D's may mean that you think many things are possible, but you're not holding your breath!**

- **6 or more A's may mean that you don't have much hope for the world—and you're probably placing a lot of limits on yourself, too.**

> **"You can't hit a home run unless you step up to the plate. You can't catch fish unless you put your line in the water. You can't reach your goals if you don't try."**
> —Kathy Seligman, journalist

PEOPLE WHO WOULDN'T LISTEN

Sometimes other people try to set limits for us. They tell us what we can and can't do, and especially what we aren't any good at. Here are some examples.

- In 1889, the editor of the *San Francisco Examiner* told Rudyard Kipling, "I'm sorry, Mr. Kipling, but you just don't know how to use the English language."

- In 1927, the head of a drama school advised a young would-be actress to "try another profession. *Any* other." The actress's name was Lucille Ball.

P.S. If you marked statement #1 with an A, read on: Charles H. Duell was Commissioner of the United States Office of Patents when he told President William McKinley, "Everything that can be invented has been invented." That was in 1899. Here are just a few of the things that have been invented since then: electric vacuum cleaner (1907), stainless steel (1916), automatic toaster (1918), elevator (1922), television (1923), rocket engine (1926), nylon (1937), jet engine (1939), radar (1940), computer (1944). Today the U.S. Patent and Trademark Office receives about 100,000 applications for patents each year.

Find Out MORE

✱ Write down three things you would like to do that seem difficult or even impossible. List the things that limit you. Put the list in a safe place, then look back at it in a few years. See if you're on your way to accomplishing those difficult or impossible things.

✱ Read biographies of people who overcame limits and went on to accomplish great things. Ask your teacher or librarian for help in finding interesting books.

- In 1954, the manager of the Grand Ole Opry in Nashville, Tennessee, fired a singer after one performance, saying, "You ain't goin' nowhere . . . son. You ought to go back to drivin' a truck." The manager was talking to Elvis Presley.

- In 1959, an executive at Universal Pictures said to actor Burt Reynolds, "You have no talent."

- In 1962, an executive of Decca Records said this about the Beatles: "We don't like their sound. Groups of guitars are on the way out."

PSI #6

BOOST YOUR MIND POWER

Ideas and thoughts have power, even over your physical body. Your beliefs can limit your horizons or expand them. When people finally started believing that the world was round, they began sailing all over the globe!

PART I:

Do the stretch illustrated in this picture. Stretch as far as you can.

Now close your eyes, relax, and imagine yourself stretching even farther. Concentrate on really "seeing" this image. Then try the stretch again.

PART II:

Close your eyes and make a mental picture of a fresh, juicy lemon. When you have a vivid picture in your mind, imagine taking a bite out of the lemon.

PART III:

Make a pendulum by tying a heavy object (like a washer) to the end of a 6"-long string. Hold the pendulum between your thumb and forefinger over the center of this square. Rest your elbow firmly on the table.

Ask a "Yes" or "No" question and concentrate on your answer. Keep your elbow on the table so you don't consciously move the pendulum to the word you're thinking.

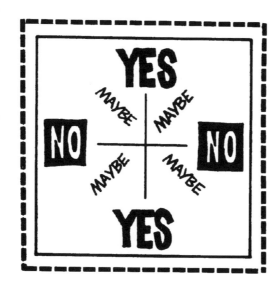

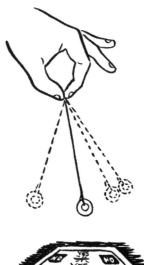

> **"All acts performed in the world begin in the imagination."**
> —*Barbara Grizzuti Harrison, writer*

WHAT'S YOUR STYLE?

After "seeing" yourself stretch, were you able to stretch farther on your second try?

YES ☐   **NO** ☐

When you "saw" yourself bite the lemon, did your mouth water?

YES ☐   **NO** ☐

When you thought of the answer to your question, did the pendulum "magically" move to the word you were thinking?

YES ☐   **NO** ☐

- If you checked YES even once, then you've felt your Mind Power in action.
- If you checked YES more than once, your Mind Power may be stronger than you know!

P.S. The reason the pendulum moved isn't magical at all. The powerful thought in your mind caused tiny muscles in your fingertips to move, even though you weren't aware that this was happening. This is called *ideomotor response*.

Find Out MORE

✳ Practice building your Mind Power to help you achieve a personal goal. Imagine yourself giving a speech in front of your class, running faster or jumping higher, writing a poem, making friends with someone you've admired from a distance, or anything else you choose.

> "As long as you can envision the fact that you can do something, you can do it—as long as you really believe it 100 percent."
>
> —Arnold Schwarzenegger, five times Mr. Universe, actor, former chairman of the President's Council on Physical Fitness and Sports, Governor of California

MIND OVER MATTER: THE POWER OF BELIEVING IN YOURSELF

- For thousands of years, people believed that it was physically impossible for a human being to run a mile in four minutes. But on May 6, 1954, Roger Bannister broke the four-minute-mile barrier. Within the next year, 37 more runners followed in his footsteps, and 300 more the year after that. Now runners do it all the time.

- When an Australian basketball team wanted to be able to shoot more baskets, the team divided into three groups.

  Group 1 practiced taking foul shots for 30 minutes every day. After 20 days, they noticed a 24 percent improvement.

  Group 2 did nothing. They noticed a 0 percent improvement.

  Group 3 practiced mentally. They didn't actually shoot baskets; they imagined themselves shooting baskets. (Just like you imagined yourself stretching even farther.)

  They noticed a 23 percent improvement—almost as much as the group that practiced for 30 minutes every day.

- The 1976 Russian Olympic Team trained in this way:

  Group A: 100% physical training, 0% mental training

  Group B: 75% physical training, 25% mental training

  Group C: 50% physical training, 50% mental training

  Group D: 25% physical training, 75% mental training

  Group D showed the most improvement.

- Other athletes who have used mental imagery for success include tennis greats Steffi Graf and Andre Agassi, Olympic champion ice skater Kristi Yamaguchi, golf pro Tiger Woods, and champion boxer Muhammad Ali.

PSI #7

WHAT DO YOU SEE?

Look at this inkblot. What do you see?

A spacecraft landing on Mars?
A princess in an elaborate headdress?
An insect? A hairpin? Something else?

There is a personality test based on what people see in inkblots. It is called the *Rorschach* test. The Rorschach test is made up of 10 large cards with inkblots printed on them. The person taking the test looks at the cards one by one in a certain order.

Psychologists believe that the Rorschach test reveals clues about your personality. How you interpret the inkblots tells the psychologist what you are looking for in life, or what is on your mind.

The Rorschach test is kept secret. The real inkblots are never printed in magazines or books. That's because the test depends on spontaneous responses to the inkblots. Psychologists don't want test-takers to know what the blots look like ahead of time.

This PSI isn't the Rorschach test, but it does use inkblots, and it asks you to tell what you see in them.

Look quickly at the inkblots numbered 1–10. If you like, turn them around or upside down. Write what you see in the spaces beside each inkblot.

1

_____

_____

_____

_____

_____

_____

2

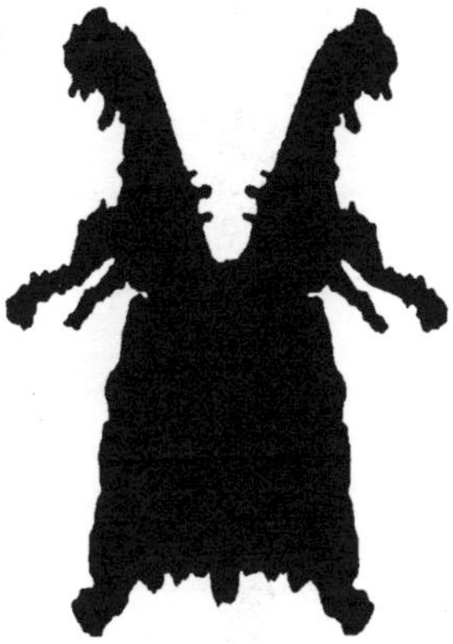

_____
_____
_____
_____
_____
_____

3

_____
_____
_____
_____
_____
_____

4

_____
_____
_____
_____
_____
_____
_____

5

6

7

8

_____

_____

_____

_____

_____

_____

9

_____

_____

_____

_____

_____

_____

_____

10

_____

_____

_____

_____

_____

_____

WHAT'S YOUR STYLE?

Here are some ways to interpret what you see in the inkblots.
Decide for yourself if they flt you.

You probably see a main image or character in each inkblot.
Where is that main image in relation to the whole inkblot?

IF YOUR MAIN IMAGE IS . . .	THIS MAY MEAN . . .
to the right of the center	you focus on the future
to the left of the center	you focus on the past
in the center	you focus on the here and now
in the dark blots	you think the way most people do
in the white spaces	you are an unusual, perhaps creative thinker
in the upper portions of the inkblot (or if you see your image moving upward)	you are an achiever
in the lower portions of the inkblot (or if you see your image falling down)	you are sad about something

What kinds of images do you see most often?

IF YOU SEE . . .	THIS MAY MEAN . . .
inanimate objects	you are good at mechanical things
abstract ideas (like joy or freedom)	you enjoy dealing with ideas
plants or animals	you are a nature lover
people	you are sociable
food	you like to take care of people or be taken care of
action	you are a doer rather than a thinker (or maybe you are both)
danger or aggression	you are angry or worried about something

WHAT OTHER PEOPLE SEE

Here are some of the things other people have seen in these inkblots. The numbers of the responses are the same as the numbers on the inkblots. In other words, the "man or monkey with cymbals" response goes with inkblot #1. Read the other nine responses, then look back at the matching inkblots. Can you see the same things?

1. man or monkey with cymbals
2. alligator or dragon
3. fork
4. flower
5. cowboy
6. reflection of a scene in water, or a man's face with a bushy beard
7. sky divers, or people holding hands
8. tree with owl, or throne
9. two circus clowns and a man in a stovepipe hat
10. ballet dancers facing one another

Find Out MORE

✱ Show these inkblots to your family, friends, or classmates. Have them write what they see. Then help them interpret their answers.

✱ Make your own inkblots. Cover your work area with a thick layer of newspapers. Fold a piece of white paper once or several times. Drop a small drop of ink in the middle or in the creases. Re-fold the paper and press the creases to spread the ink. Open it and there's your inkblot!

"The art of becoming wise is the art of knowing what to overlook."
—William James, psychologist

HOW MANY PERSONAS DO YOU HAVE?

PSI #8

A persona is an image you show the outside world. It is like a mask you wear to fit the occasion. In fact, the word "persona" comes from the Latin *per sonara,* which means "to speak through"— a reference to the masks actors once wore and "spoke through."

If we didn't have personas, we would act the same way all the time. A doctor would go home from the office and act like a doctor with his or her own family. Or a doctor would go to the office and act like a parent with his or her patients.

Most people have at least two personas: a public one, and a private one. The persona they use depends on where they are, what they are doing, and who they are with. Some of your personas may be "friend," "student," "sister," or "son." Each of your personas is made up of your real qualities, but it also hides some qualities you don't want other people to see. The persona you show your teachers may not have a temper. The persona you show your baseball team may never cry.

Read this list of behaviors. Check the ones you sometimes do. Then look at the list of people in your life on the next page. Next to each behavior, write the name or names of the people who would be very surprised to see you do that particular thing.

1. Become very quiet. ☐

_____

_____

2. Start an argument. ☐

_____

_____

3. Brag about your grades. ☐

_____

_____

4. Break up a fight. ☐

_____

_____

5. Show your temper. ☐

_____

_____

6. Cry about something. ☐

_____

_____

7. Talk a lot. ☐

_____

_____

8. Finish your school work or chores on time. ☐

_____

_____

9. Act really silly. ☐

_____

_____

_____

10. Give in to someone. ☐

_____

_____

People in your life:

Mother   Father   Brother   Sister   Friends   Teacher   Grandparents

Any others?

_____   _____
_____   _____
_____   _____
_____   _____

WHAT'S YOUR STYLE?

HOW MANY OF THE BEHAVIORS DID YOU CHECK?

HOW MANY PEOPLE DID YOU LIST?

(Count 1 for each time you listed a person. For example, listing "Grandfather, teacher, best friend" by a behavior would count as 3.)

- If you listed lots of people, chances are you have many personas.

- If you listed few people, you probably tend to show more people the "real you."

A persona may be positive—a good student, an artist, a loving son or daughter. Or a persona may be negative—a bully, a know-it-all, a troublemaker. Sometimes people hide behind a persona because they're afraid other people won't like them the way they are. Their "masks" keep people from getting to know them.

But personas can also be very helpful. Politicians and celebrities use personas to protect their private and family lives from the public. Society uses them to set standards for behavior, dress, and interactions between people. When everyone has more-or-less the same idea of how things should be (how bosses should act toward employees, how teachers should act toward students), relationships go more smoothly.

Whatever your personas may be, they're all part of your personal style.

"All the world's a stage,
And all the men and women merely players:
They have their exits and their entrances;
And one man in his time plays many parts..."

—*William Shakespeare*, As You Like It

Find Out MORE

* Ask your parents to describe the personas they have. They may wear different "masks" around you, the people they work with, their adult friends, or their own parents.

* Pick two to five situations that are common in your life (such as school, home, an athletic team, a club, a church). Do you have different personas for some of these? If yes, describe them.

* Make a mask showing your favorite persona—the one you wish people could see all the time.

* Imagine a world without personas, where everyone said and did exactly what they felt like all the time. Would you like to live in this kind of world? Why or why not?

MULTIPLE PERSONALITIES

Some people confuse having different personas with having "multiple personalities." Personas are healthy ways of dealing with variety in our lives. Having multiple personalities is a rare mental disorder that can be diagnosed by a doctor.

If you think you have too many personas, or you think they're too different from the real you, talk to an adult. Talking to someone you trust may help you get rid of a "mask" or two so people can see the real you.

PSI #9

THUMB THEORIES

People have come up with all sorts of ways to test personality. One of these is reading the shapes of fingers and thumbs—kind of like palm reading. These are not scientific ways of testing personality, but they can be a lot of fun!

Make a fist with the hand you DON'T write with.

Which picture looks like your fist?

WHAT'S YOUR STYLE?

- If your thumb is on the inside of your fist (picture 1), you may be unsure of yourself and uncomfortable with other people. You may be reluctant to "take the first punch." You tend to hold in your anger.

- If your thumb is on the outside of your fist (picture 2), you may get angry easily. You probably have a strong will and are usually "on top of things."

Find Out MORE

✶ Just for fun, develop your own theory for testing personality using another part of the body. For example, you could count the hairs on each knuckle, analyze eyelashes, compare the length of the leg to the length of the arm, or anything else you decide. Test your theory on your family and friends.

MORE "RULES OF THUMB"

- If your thumb curves in, you may think before making decisions.
- If your thumb is straight and thick, you use intuition to solve problems, and you may be stubborn.
- If you have a long thumb, you may like giving directions.
- If you have a short thumb, you may prefer being told what to do.

PSI #10

WHAT SORT OF MORPH ARE YOU?

Another theory of personality has to do with your body size and shape. Psychologist William Sheldon divided bodies into three basic types. An **endomorph** is a heavy-set person. A **mesomorph** is a muscular or athletic person. An **ectomorph** is a thin person.

Look at these three pictures.
Check the one that seems closest to your body type.

1 ☐   2 ☐   3 ☐

Now read each pair of words.
Circle the word or phrase from each pair that seems closest to your personality.

HAPPY **or** WORRIED

LOVES PEOPLE **or** LIKES TO BE ALONE

COMPETITIVE **or** NOT COMPETITIVE

SEEKS PLEASURE **or** SEEKS ACTION

RELAXED **or** NERVOUS

WHAT'S YOUR STYLE?

HERE IS WHAT THE THEORY SAYS:

- An endomorph is happy, relaxed, loves people, and seeks pleasure.
- A mesomorph is action-seeking and competitive.
- An ectomorph is nervous, worried, and likes to be alone.

DO YOU AGREE WITH THE THEORY? IS IT TRUE FOR YOU?

Famous Morphs

Fill in the blanks with more morphs you know about.

Endomorphs: Cookie Monster, Santa Claus, Winnie the Pooh,

_____

_____

_____ ?

Mesomorphs: Superman, Popeye, Tigger,

_____

_____

_____ ?

Ectomorphs: C-3PO, Bert from Sesame Street,

_____

_____

_____ ?

Find Out MORE

✱ How does your body type affect your personal style? How does it influence the kinds of choices you make for yourself?

✱ Is there something about your body you don't like that keeps you from doing things you wish you could do?

✱ If you feel comfortable, talk about your body with an adult you trust. Adults have lived in their bodies a long time. They may know things about bodies and personalities that you might want to hear.

CAUTION! THEORY AT WORK!

Some theories about personality and behavior have been established by tests and research. Many people agree with them and think they are useful.

But all theories are just that—theories. Some haven't yet been proved correct or incorrect. Theories may be fun, and sometimes they may be useful, but you're always free to say, "Hey, wait a minute! I don't agree with this theory at all."

WHAT DO DOODLES DO?

Jim and Allison have equal athletic abilities. But Jim is happy just to play soccer, while Allison has the feeling that she must be the "star player." Allison and Jim also have equal intellectual abilities. But Allison is perfectly contented getting C's, while Jim pushes himself to get A's. The two friends have different needs to achieve in these two areas.

Psychologists have found that they can measure a person's need for achievement, or "nAch," by looking at the way he or she doodles. Most people have a different nAch at different times of their lives, and for different activities. But some people may have a high nAch all the time. This PSI measures your nAch at different times. CAUTION: DON'T look at the "What's Your Style?" scoring section until you have done ALL of the doodles, or your score won't be valid.

1. Doodle here NOW:

2. Do your favorite physical activity for 10 minutes. Then doodle in this space:

3. Call a friend on the phone.
   Doodle in this space while you're talking to your friend:

4. Doodle in this space when you first get up in the morning:

5. Doodle in this space right before you go to bed at night:

WHAT'S YOUR STYLE?

Give yourself a +1, a -1, or a 0, depending on how you doodled. **HINT:** If you're not sure how to score part of a doodle, just give it a 0.

A. If you filled the space in the doodle box, give yourself a +1. If you didn't fill the space, give yourself a 0.

SCORE:

| BOX 1 | BOX 2 | BOX 3 | BOX 4 | BOX 5 |

B. If your doodle included cubes, give yourself a -1 for each cube you made. If your doodle didn't include any cubes, give yourself a 0.

SCORE:

| BOX 1 | BOX 2 | BOX 3 | BOX 4 | BOX 5 |

C. Count the number of diagonal lines you doodled.

DIAGONAL LINES:

| BOX 1 | BOX 2 | BOX 3 | BOX 4 | BOX 5 |

Now count the number of vertical and horizontal lines you doodled.

VERTICAL AND HORIZONTAL LINES:

| BOX 1 | BOX 2 | BOX 3 | BOX 4 | BOX 5 |

If you doodled more diagonal lines than vertical and horizontal lines, give yourself a +1. If not, give yourself a 0.

SCORE:

| BOX 1 | BOX 2 | BOX 3 | BOX 4 | BOX 5 |

D. Count the number of S-shapes you doodled (backward or forward), and give yourself a +1 for each.

SCORE:

| BOX 1 | BOX 2 | BOX 3 | BOX 4 | BOX 5 |

E. Look for wavy lines. Give yourself a 0 for each time you doodled a single wave, like this:

Give yourself a -1 for each time you doodled more than one wave connected together, like this:

SCORE:

| BOX 1 | BOX 2 | BOX 3 | BOX 4 | BOX 5 |

F. Total your scores for each doodle box. (Remember that you may be adding positive and negative numbers together.)

| BOX 1 TOTAL | BOX 2 TOTAL | BOX 3 TOTAL | BOX 4 TOTAL | BOX 5 TOTAL |

Now add these totals together to get your nAch score:

nAch SCORE: _____

The more pluses you have, the higher your need to achieve. The more minuses you have, the lower your need to achieve.

- +35 and above nAch = a VERY high need to achieve

- +20 to +30 nAch = a high need to achieve

- +5 to +15 nAch = a somewhat high need to achieve

- 0 nAch = neutral; you don't especially feel the need to achieve, but neither are you reluctant to achieve

- -5 to -15 nAch = a somewhat low need to achieve

- -20 to -30 nAch = a low need to achieve

- -35 or more nAch = a VERY low need to achieve

The scoring for this PSI is rather complicated. If you're feeling confused, here are two examples of how doodle boxes were scored. Can you see how Doodle X shows a higher need to achieve than Doodle Y?

DOODLE X

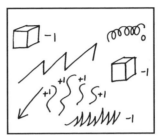

DOODLE Y

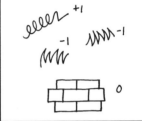

DOODLE X	DOODLE Y
A. Fill space? YES = +1	A. Fill space? NO = 0
B. Cubes? 2 = -2	B. Cubes? NONE = 0
C. More diagonal lines? YES = +1	C. More diagonal lines? NO = 0
D. S-shapes? 4 = +4	D. S-shapes? 1 = +1
E. Connected wavy-line doodles? 1 = -1	E. Connected wavy-line doodles? 2 = -2
F. **TOTAL:** +3 nAch	F. **TOTAL:** -1 nAch

Find Out MORE

✱ Psychologist Elliot Aronson has studied the relationship between doodles and the need for achievement. He has found that high nAchievers are likely to draw lots of single, unattached lines, while low nAchievers are likely to draw connected, overlaid, or "blotchy" lines. Look back at your doodle boxes. Does this make sense for you?

✱ Find out about different cultures by looking at their art. Pay attention to the different types of lines used on pottery, in paintings, in silverware, or in furniture design. Make a judgment based on what you see, then check it out by reading more about the culture.

✱ Does recess help people feel more like achieving? Find out by designing an experiment. You might give a "doodle test" before and after recesses. (In Japan and China, students are given a recess after each class to increase their attention span and help them relax.)

PSI #12

WHAT DOES YOUR SIGNATURE SAY ABOUT YOU?

Did you know that your handwriting can tell you something about your personality? The study of handwriting is called *graphology.* Graphologists analyze people's handwriting. Businesses hire graphologists to study the handwriting of people they are thinking about hiring. Police departments hire graphologists to look at notes left by criminals. Not everybody thinks that graphology is reliable. But almost everybody agrees that it's fun.

Sign your full name here:

_____

WHAT'S YOUR STYLE?

Study your signature. Then circle each phrase under "What You See" that describes your writing. Read the explanations under "What This Says About You" to learn what your signature says about your personality.

WHAT YOU SEE	WHAT THIS SAYS ABOUT YOU
Large Large writing	You think big; you like to be noticed
small Small writing	You're detail-oriented; you don't like to be in the public eye
right Writing that slants right	You like to show your feelings; you're sociable, active, and forward-moving

WHAT YOU SEE	WHAT THIS SAYS ABOUT YOU
left Writing that slants left	You keep your emotions to yourself; you're unwilling to go out and "face the world"
optimistic Writing that slants up	You're optimistic
tired, sad Writing that slants down	You're tired or sad about something

WHAT YOU SEE | WHAT THIS SAYS ABOUT YOU

Neutral
Upright writing
> You're neutral and unemotional about many issues; you're self-reliant, calm, and in control of yourself

unpredictable
Writing with varying slants
> You're unpredictable; you haven't yet decided where you want to go in life (many teenagers have this kind of writing)

narrow
Narrow writing
> You tend to be economical and hold "narrow" views about things

Broad
Narrow writing
> You're somewhat uncontrollable; you like room to think and move freely

Heavy
Dark writing (from heavy pressure)
> You're determined and action-oriented; you feel "under pressure" to get things done

light
Light writing (from light pressure)
> You dislike violence, loud noises, and bright lights; you're sensitive, tender, and perceptive

WHAT YOU SEE | WHAT THIS SAYS ABOUT YOU

disconnected
Disconnected letters
> You concentrate on details instead of the "big picture"; you have original ideas

connected
Connected letters
> You like logic and order; you're good at understanding relationships and the way things "connect" to one another

wide spaces
Wide spaces between words
> You need space; sometimes you seem standoffish. You are clear-headed and have an uncluttered mind.

narrow spaces
Narrow spaces between words
> You're a very sociable person who enjoys "getting together" with a lot of people

Creative
Unusual ways of crossing T's and dotting I's
> You're a creative person

Open minded
Open O's and P's
> You're open-minded

Do you agree or disagree with the explanations? Did you discover anything new about yourself?

Find Out MORE

✽ Borrow a book on graphology from the library. Analyze your own writing, then analyze your friends' and family's writing. Tell them what their signatures say and ask if they agree with your analysis.

✽ Write your signature on a piece of paper and put it away in a safe place. Look at it again a few years from now. Has your signature changed? Have you changed?

FAMOUS SIGNATURES MATCH-UP

Identify these famous signatures after reading their descriptions. The answers are printed upside down at the end.

1. The top of his "t" streaks away like a comet; it travels at the speed of light. His "A" is a star in the sky!

2. With grace and poise, his signature "dances" across the page. You can see the music in his heart by the treble clef that dances overhead.

3. His signature goes down in a depressed way and has rigid and cutting marks. The capital "H" almost has a swastika in it.

4. You can see in his name the rocket ready to launch. There is even a launching pad in the final "g."

5. His signature has the obvious markings of a ball player. The letters are rounded, and there is even a "goal."

6. Here is someone who might like recognition for his brilliant ideas. The big loop connects the first and last name and resembles a phonograph record.

1. Albert Einstein, genius and mathematician, developed the Theory of Relativity; **2.** Fred Astaire, American dancer and movie star; **3.** Adolf Hitler, German dictator; **4.** Neil Armstrong, American astronaut, first man to walk on the moon; **5.** Pele, Brazilian soccer player; **6.** Thomas Alva Edison, American inventor of the telegraph, microphone, incandescent light, and much more

YOUR COLORFUL PERSONALITY

Colors often remind people of different qualities. Maybe red makes you think of anger, or blue makes you think of peace. Some people believe that your favorite color says something about your personality.

PART I: Write the name of your favorite color here: _____

Write one thing you think your favorite color says about you:

_____

Match the colors with the personality traits you think they represent.

COLORS	PERSONALITY TRAITS
Red	A. Patient and persistent. Poised and dignified. A rational decision-maker.
Green	B. Intellectual and spiritual. Wise and high-minded. Inventive and creative.
Orange	C. Tradition and authority are important. A solid citizen, admired by many.
Blue	D. Courageous, energetic, enthusiastic, restless. Passionate and impulsive!
Yellow	E. Sensitive and refined. High standards. Has a devoted circle of close friends.
Purple	F. Warm nature. Filled with the joy of life. Inspires others to reach their highest potential. Popular; a leader.

PART II: How does each of these colors make you feel? What does it make you think of? Write the first answers that come to mind.

RED

_____

_____

GREEN

_____

_____

ORANGE

_____

_____

BLUE

_____

_____

YELLOW

_____

_____

PURPLE

_____

_____

PART III: Color each of the shapes below with one of these six colors: red, orange, yellow, green, blue, purple. (Decide which shape "looks" yellow, blue, etc., to you.)

WHAT'S YOUR STYLE?

PART I: Most people match up the colors and personality traits like this:

Red: D
Green: C
Orange: F
Blue: A
Yellow: B
Purple: E

What's your favorite color? Do the personality traits for that color fit you? If they don't, then Part I of this PSI isn't true for you. That's okay. Color can still tell you about your personal style.

PART II: Color can make us feel certain ways. For example, orange is believed to make people hungry. (That's why so many fast-food restaurants are painted orange inside.) Bubblegum pink is believed to calm people down. (It has been used in prisons.)

There's a scientific explanation for how color affects our feelings. Each color has a particular wavelength. When it strikes the color-sensitive cones at the back of the eye, the cells fire, sending nerve signals to the brain. This may release certain brain chemicals which determine our moods.

There's no right or wrong way to respond to color. Orange may make you feel hungry—or it may make you feel too nervous to eat. The way you feel about color is part of your personal style.

PART III: Ask a friend or family member to do this coloring exercise, too. Compare your answers. How are they alike? How are they different? Remember that there's no right or wrong way to feel about color.

"What a joyous thing is color! How influenced we all are by it, even if we are unconscious of how our sense of restfulness has been brought about."

—*Elsie De Wolfe, actress and writer*

Find Out MORE

✱ What's your favorite color for each of these things?

winter sweater

_____

summer sweater

_____

your car (pretend you have one)

_____

your parents' car

_____

your house

_____

your room

_____

your school

_____

your bike

_____

your pet

_____

your favorite jacket

_____

✱ Experiment with color in your own room. For one week, put a colored sheet over your window, or a colored shade on a lamp. At the end of the week, write about how it felt to live with that color. Try different colors until you find one you really like.

✱ What was your favorite color last year?

COLOR RESPONSE SURVEY

Find out how other people respond to color.

Take a survey! ➤

Invite six people to participate in your survey. Use the chart on the next page. Write their names in the boxes in the left-hand column. Then ask them how they feel about each of the colors in the other six columns. Record their responses.

COLOR RESPONSE SURVEY

Name of Person	Black	White	Red	Blue	Yellow	Green

MOOD MUSIC

Do you ever get in the mood to hear a certain kind of music? Has music ever cheered you up, made you sad, or made you feel like dancing? Does the same music sound different to you when you're in different moods? Music communicates feeling. Some psychologists think music affects us because it reminds us of things that have happened in our lives. A certain song might trigger a memory of something good or bad.

Other psychologists think our responses to music are inborn. For instance, almost all people think high-pitched music is happy and low-pitched music is sad. Most people hear a fast tempo as lively and a slow tempo as relaxing. These responses to music are almost universal.

Another theory is that we respond to music because of rhythms in our bodies (our breathing, our heartbeat) or chemicals in our brain. Psychologist Howard Gardner has noticed two things about patients who have suffered damage to certain parts of their brains: They are often very unemotional, and they rarely care about music.

Since music affects our emotions, it's sometimes used for therapy. Music has been used to treat sick people, alcohol and other drug abusers, and heart patients. Advertisers and movie producers know how powerful music can be. They use it to make you feel a certain way about their products or their films.

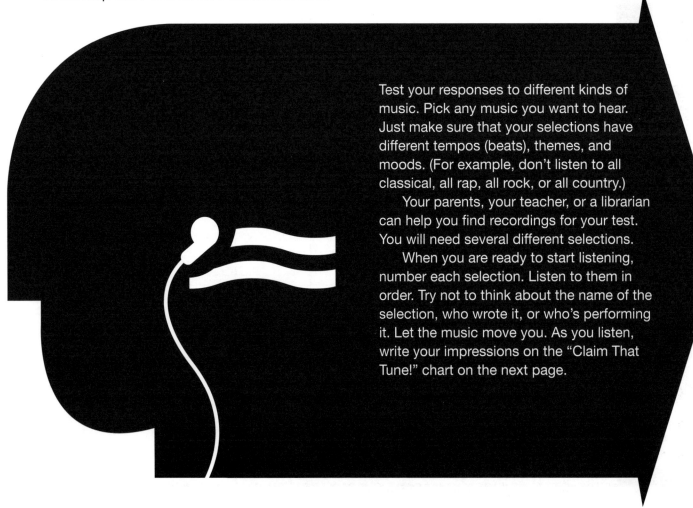

Test your responses to different kinds of music. Pick any music you want to hear. Just make sure that your selections have different tempos (beats), themes, and moods. (For example, don't listen to all classical, all rap, all rock, or all country.)

Your parents, your teacher, or a librarian can help you find recordings for your test. You will need several different selections.

When you are ready to start listening, number each selection. Listen to them in order. Try not to think about the name of the selection, who wrote it, or who's performing it. Let the music move you. As you listen, write your impressions on the "Claim That Tune!" chart on the next page.

CLAIM THAT TUNE!

YOUR FEELINGS

Selection #	Color	Historical Time	Country	People	Event	Season/Time of Year	Feeling	Other Comments

WHAT'S YOUR STYLE?

Music can do many things. It can make you want to dance or cry. It can make you feel religious or patriotic, calm or excited, sleepy or full of energy.

What kinds of music do you like best? How do you like to feel? The music you like is part of your personal style. You don't have to limit yourself only to the music your friends like, or music that's currently popular.

What's one of your favorite kinds of music? How does it make you feel?

> *"Just as nutritionists advise eating a well-balanced diet, I recommend that people include a balanced sound diet in any personal well-being program."*
> —Steven Halpern, composer, producer, and recording artist

Find Out MORE

✱ Do "Claim That Tune!" in a group, then compare responses.

✱ Invite a friend over, then draw a scene or design while listening to the same piece of music. (Music without words may work best.) Afterward, compare your drawings. Did the music suggest the same thing to both of you?

✱ Play different selections for your pet. Does your pet seem to prefer any particular kind of music?

✱ Rent a movie and watch a scene that has a particular kind of music (maybe the theme, or a popular song). Now rewind and play the same scene over again—only this time, turn down the sound and play another kind of music of your choice. How does this change the mood of the scene? (For example, you're watching a scary movie and you play a silly song...or you're watching a cartoon and you play part of a symphony.)

✱ Start collecting music you like. As your collection grows, notice how your musical tastes change.

> *"Music has been my playmate...and my crying towel."*
> —Buffy Sainte-Marie, songwriter, singer, and civil rights activist

MOOD FOOD

PSI #15

Food can affect your feelings. Of course, you know you feel miserable if you eat too much or if you are very hungry. But there are other ways that food can set the mood. Hot soup or hot chocolate on a cold day can make you feel cozy. Cotton candy can remind you of a carnival and make you feel happy. An apple or a carrot stick can make you feel fit even before it has had the chance to do its good deeds for your health.

Read each of the food categories on the next two pages and think of foods that fit them. (These can be your favorites, or foods you hate—it's up to you.) Write down the foods you think of. Imagine yourself eating them. Then write down how each food makes you feel. Try to come up with lots of different words to describe your feelings.

> **"It's odd how large a part food plays in the memories of childhood. There are grown men and women who still shudder at the sight of spinach, or turn away with loathing from stewed prunes and tapioca...Luckily, however, it's the good tastes one remembers best."**
>
> —*Caroline Lejeune, film critic and playwright*

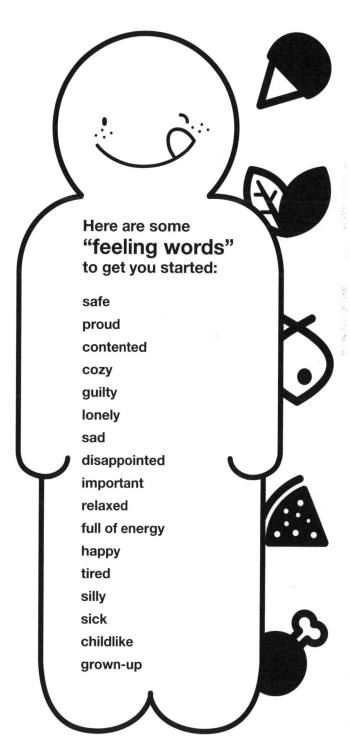

Here are some "feeling words" to get you started:

- **safe**
- **proud**
- **contented**
- **cozy**
- **guilty**
- **lonely**
- **sad**
- **disappointed**
- **important**
- **relaxed**
- **full of energy**
- **happy**
- **tired**
- **silly**
- **sick**
- **childlike**
- **grown-up**

FOODS

Cold -

_____

_____

Hot (temperature) -

_____

_____

Crunchy -

_____

_____

"Fast" -

_____

_____

"Fun" -

_____

_____

"Health" -

_____

_____

Holiday/special occasion -

_____

_____

Seasonal (foods you eat in the spring, -
summer, fall, winter)

_____

_____

Time-related (foods you eat in the morning, for
lunch, for bedtime snacks, on the weekends) -

_____

_____

Place-related (foods you eat at the circus, movies,
ball game, carnival) -

_____

_____

FOOD MOODS

_____

_____

_____

_____

_____

_____

_____

_____

_____

_____

_____

_____

_____

_____

_____

_____

_____

_____

_____

_____

_____

_____

_____

_____

WHAT'S YOUR STYLE?

Many people like the same foods. But you're you—a unique individual. Maybe your friends like candy bars, but all that chocolate gives you a headache. Maybe you like salt on your oatmeal. Maybe you snack on spinach! The foods you like and the ways they affect you are part of your personal style.

Find Out MORE

* Plan a family meal of foods that make you feel good. (Try to include at least one healthful dish.)

* Plan a special meal for somebody's birthday...with all of that person's feel-good foods.

* Keep a diary of what you eat for three days. Write down how you feel before and after each meal or snack. What do you eat when you're feeling lonely? What do you eat when you're feeling tired?

* Survey your friends to find out what unusual food combinations they like. (Scrambled eggs and mustard? Pickles and oatmeal?) Try some of their "recipes."

* Eat dinner for breakfast and breakfast for dinner. (Who says you can't start your day with spaghetti or end it with granola?)

* Make a list of foods you like best. Make another list of foods you hate most. Keep your lists to look at in a few years. Have your tastes changed?

FOOD SCENTS & SIGHTS

The way food smells is a big part of the way it affects you. (Try holding your nose and eating something...you won't taste a thing!)

Yale University psychologists Gary Schwartz and Tyler Lorig have done interesting research on this subject. They asked 16 students to sniff three scents for one minute. The scents were Spiced Apple, Eucalyptus, and Lavender. While the students were sniffing, Schwartz and Lorig measured their brain-wave activity. They found a connection between Spiced Apple scent and increased alpha waves in the brain. When we're relaxed, the brain emits alpha waves. So, it seemed that sniffing Spiced Apple made the students feel relaxed.

Why? Maybe it's because people take deeper breaths when they're enjoying a scent—deep breathing is known to cause relaxation. Or maybe focusing on a scent keeps you too busy to think about your problems. Or maybe...(do you have any ideas?).

Schwartz and Lorig asked the students to just imagine the scent. Even then, their alpha waves increased! So, the next time you need to relax, think....SPICED APPLES.

The way food looks also affects your feelings. Some young children were asked to eat food that had been dyed with a harmless blue food coloring. The children became ill after eating the blue potatoes.

Why? Maybe it's because people have a built-in reaction to funny-colored foods. Often, spoiled foods turn moldy blue-green. This could be something humans learned a long time ago as a way to protect themselves against food poisoning. Can you think of any other reasons?

If you read the book *Green Eggs and Ham* by Dr. Seuss when you were younger, you may have wondered what it would be like to eat green eggs. You could make some by adding a few drops of green food coloring to raw eggs before scrambling them. Do you think you would want to eat them? Why or why not?

TIME OUT

CAN PHRENOLOGY HELP YOU GET A-HEAD?

Phrenology (fri-NÄL-uh-jee) is the study of the shape of the skull, especially the bumps. It was started by Fran Joseph Gall and Johann Kaspar, two 19th-century researchers. They believed that phrenology was a way to learn about people's personalities and mental abilities.

Soon phrenology became so popular that even respected scientists thought it was the wave of the future. In 1899, British biologist Alfred Russel Wallace predicted, "[Phrenology] will prove to be the true science of the mind. Its practical uses in education, in self-disciplining, in reformatory treatment of criminals, and in the remedial treatment of the insane, will give it one of the highest places in the hierarchy of the sciences."

That's not how things worked out. Today, hardly anybody believes in phrenology anymore. But it's still fun to learn about. And it's possible that phrenology helped pave the way for real personality testing—much like astrology led to astronomy, and alchemy to chemistry.

Phrenology got people thinking about studying the human mind. This resulted in some interesting ideas. For example:

- The mind, like a muscle, needs exercise.
- Children learn better by doing than by studying.
- Schools should allow more free play.
- Shorter school days are better for learning.
- Physical education is important to learning.
- Punishment shouldn't be used in schools.
- Repetition drills don't help people learn.

Scientists today know much more about the brain than Gall and Kaspar did. (Although there's still a lot to learn!) Studying skulls and bumps seems like a silly thing to do.

Or is it? Take a look at the two maps on the next page. One is an old-fashioned phrenologist's brain map. The other is a modern-day neurologist's brain map. (A neurologist is a scientist who studies the brain and nervous system.) Do the maps have anything in common?

PHRENOLOGIST'S MAP

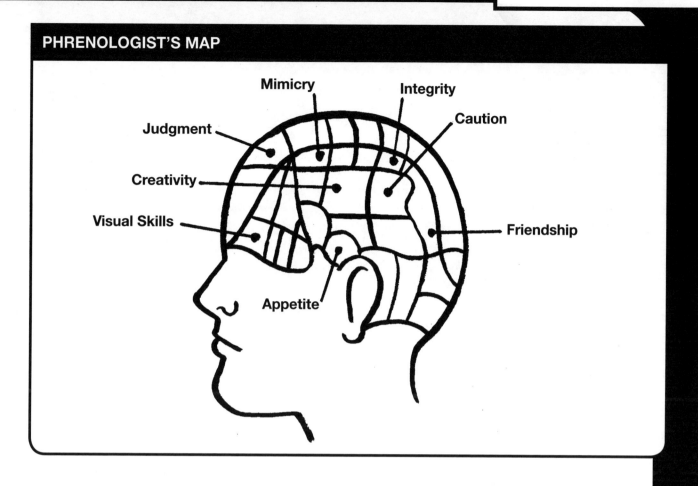

NEUROLOGIST'S MAP

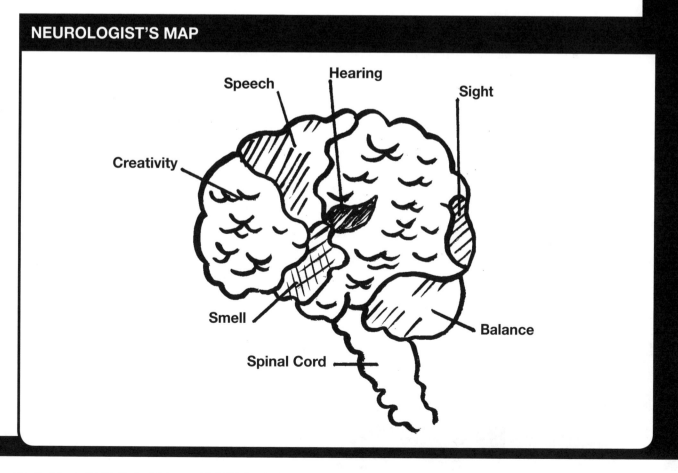

PSI #16

WHAT MAKES YOU ACT THE WAY YOU DO?

Without something to make it go, a machine just sits there. Humans make machines go—but what makes humans go? Psychologists have been working on finding answers to this question for a long time. The certain something that makes you go is called *motivation.* Motivation makes you *move.* Psychologists say that there are two types of motivation. Motivation from outside yourself is called *extrinsic.* Motivation from inside yourself is called *intrinsic.*

Read each question, then circle A or B for the option that you would most likely choose.

1. You are offered two roles in the school play. Which one will you choose?

   A. the lead role, which is glamorous and gets you a lot of attention

   B. another part that's less glamorous but lets you use more of your acting skills

2. You are offered two jobs. Which one will you choose?

   A. the one that pays very good money

   B. the one you'd really love doing, even though the pay isn't very good

3. You are choosing between two classes. Which one will you sign up for?

   A. the easier one

   B. the more interesting, more challenging one

4. You must read at least one book this semester. Which will you choose?

   A. one book from the list the teacher has given you

   B. five books of your own choosing that are just as long

5. Two people have invited you out. Which will you choose?

   A. the person who is most fashionable to be seen with

   B. the much more interesting but less popular person

6. Which do you feel you learn more from?

   A. studying for a class so you can get an A

   B. studying for a class because you're interested in it

7. In deciding between two sports, which will you choose?

   A. the one that gives trophies to the best players at the end of the season

   B. the one that's the most fun

8. Which feels better to you?

   A. cleaning your room so you will get your allowance

   B. cleaning your room because you want to

9. In general, which is more important to your decision-making?

   A. appearances

   B. meaning

10. In general, which are you more interested in?

   A. quantity

   B. quality

WHAT'S YOUR STYLE?
TOTAL YOUR A'S AND B'S.

A'S [   ]   B'S [   ]

- If you scored 8 or more A's, you're probably motivated from the outside. You care a lot about what people think of you.

- If you scored 8 or more B's, you're probably motivated from the inside. You care more about your own opinion of yourself.

Sometimes it helps to be motivated from both the inside and the outside. You can care what other people think and still be true to yourself.

Find Out MORE

✱ Think about what motivates you. Is it other people's opinions? Your own opinions? Fear? A desire to be first and best? Do your motivations help you reach your goals?

✱ Think about projects you've completed in the last few weeks. These might be school assignments, or practicing your saxophone for the band concert, or helping your sister set up her model train. What motivated you to finish them?

A LESSON IN MOTIVATION

Educator Maria Montessori believed that it's an insult to reward someone for learning. Learning is its own reward, she said; giving a reward on top of that implies that learning is just work.

Psychologists have discovered that Maria Montessori may have been right. When experimenters tried rewarding people for something they enjoyed doing, soon the people didn't like doing it as much.

One young girl figured that out on her own. Here is her story.

THE CASE OF THE HIDDEN SCHOOL BOOKS

There once was a young girl who had a very troubling problem. Three boys in her class got great pleasure from hiding her school books from her. She tried to reason with them, but it didn't work. She tried to ignore them, but they still hid her books. Finally one day she had an idea.

She told the boys that she really liked the fact that they hid her books, because it gave her a good excuse for not doing her homework. "But," she complained, "I still have to do my handwriting practice. If you will take my notebook as well as my other books, I will pay you a quarter each day."

The boys thought this sounded great. Each day they happily hid all of her books and her notebook, and she gave them a quarter. This went on for three days. On the fourth day she explained that she would have to start giving them only 15 cents because her allowance was running low. On the seventh day she told them she could only give them a nickel per day.

The boys looked at her in disgust and said, "No way! Just forget it. If you think we're going to do all of this for just a nickel a day, you're crazy!" They stopped hiding the girl's school books. Her problem had been solved.

SETTING PRIORITIES

Some things that motivate us are simple, like hunger, thirst, and sleep. Other things are more complex, like revenge, security, or recognition. Psychologist Abraham Maslow thought that people were motivated by *needs.* When one type of need was met, the person would be motivated by the next higher need. Maslow called his theory a "Hierarchy of Needs."

According to Maslow's theory, needs on the lower levels must be met before needs on the higher levels become important. For example, if you have not eaten for a week, you won't care much about love and acceptance. The goal of the hierarchy—the highest-level need—is to *self-actualize.* Self-actualized people feel that life has a purpose. Because all of their needs are met, they can help other people.

Abraham Maslow's Hierarchy of Needs

Maslow thought in terms of needs, but we can also use his theory to think about priorities.

Self-Actualization Needs: To realize our potential

Aesthetic Needs: To have beauty, symmetry, and order in our lives

Cognitive Needs: To know, understand, and explore

Self-Esteem Needs: To achieve, to gain approval and recognition from others for our achievements

Belongingness and Love Needs: To love and be loved, have relationships and be accepted

Safety Needs: To feel safe, secure, out of danger

Basic Needs: To have food, water, rest

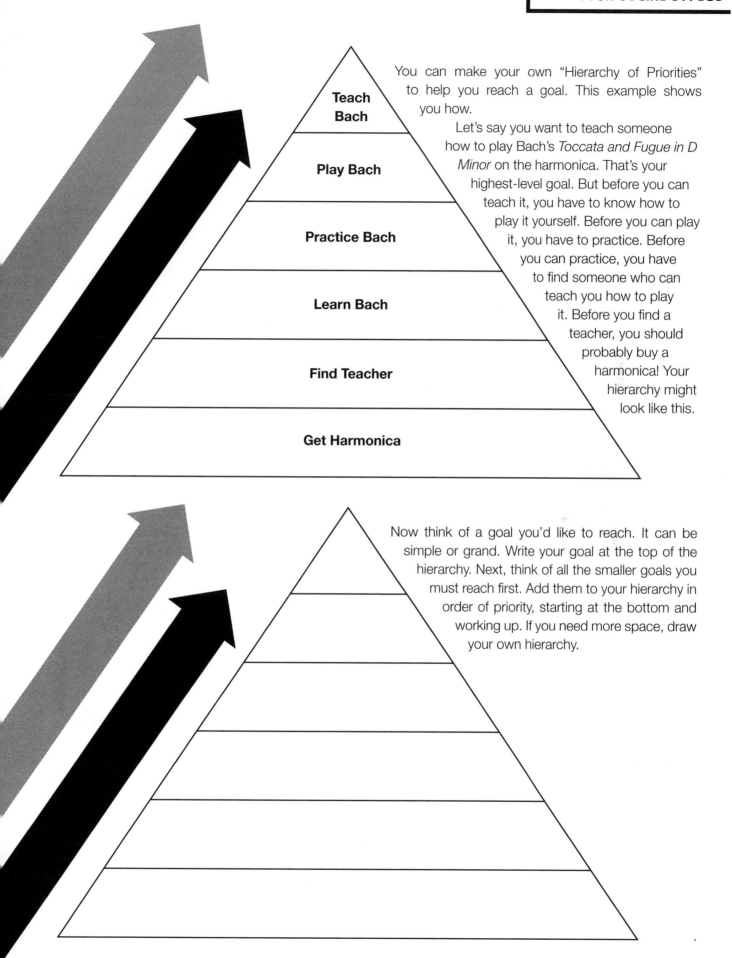

You can make your own "Hierarchy of Priorities" to help you reach a goal. This example shows you how.

Let's say you want to teach someone how to play Bach's *Toccata and Fugue in D Minor* on the harmonica. That's your highest-level goal. But before you can teach it, you have to know how to play it yourself. Before you can play it, you have to practice. Before you can practice, you have to find someone who can teach you how to play it. Before you find a teacher, you should probably buy a harmonica! Your hierarchy might look like this.

Teach Bach

Play Bach

Practice Bach

Learn Bach

Find Teacher

Get Harmonica

Now think of a goal you'd like to reach. It can be simple or grand. Write your goal at the top of the hierarchy. Next, think of all the smaller goals you must reach first. Add them to your hierarchy in order of priority, starting at the bottom and working up. If you need more space, draw your own hierarchy.

WHAT'S YOUR STYLE?

Understanding the things that motivate us can help us set priorities. Setting priorities can help us reach our goals.

How good are you at setting priorities? At reaching goals? Was this PSI hard for you to do, or easy? Was it work, or was it fun?

What do your answers to these questions tell you about your personal style?

"Rational beliefs bring us closer to getting good results in the real world."

—*Albert Ellis, psychologist*

Find Out MORE

* Pick a school subject you'd like to do better in. Ask your teacher to help you set a goal. Then set some priorities for reaching your goal.

* Think of a goal for your family. It might be something simple, like cleaning out the garage together. Work with your family to set priorities for getting the job done.

ARE YOU HABIT-BOUND?

Gravity and habit are two powerful forces in our lives. One keeps us from flying off into space. The other keeps us from having to think through everything we do. Habit tells us how to get dressed in the morning, how to study, how to find our way to the school cafeteria, and much more. We depend on habit to help us get things done. Imagine what life would be like if you had to do everything for the first time, every time you did it! Habit can also keep us from thinking of better ways to do things. Habits are so comfortable that it's easy to get into a rut. We do useless things just because "we've always done it that way."

Some habits are good; some aren't so good. And some we don't even realize we have.

For this PSI, you'll need a stopwatch or a timer to track how long it takes you to answer each group of four questions. Do questions 1–4 first, then stop and record your time. Reset the timer before you start questions 5–8.

1. Say the alphabet as quickly as you can.

2. Write your name: _____

3. Write: "San Francisco is in the United States of America." _____

_____

4. Say the months of the year in order, starting with January.

RECORD YOUR TIME for questions 1–4:

5. Say the alphabet backward as quickly as you can.

6. Write your name backward: _____

7. Write: "San Francisco is in the United States of America," but don't dot any i's, cross any t's, or capitalize anything.

_____

_____

8. Say the months of the year backward, starting with December.

RECORD YOUR TIME for questions 5–8:

WHAT'S YOUR STYLE?

Subtract your first time (for questions 1–4) from your second time (questions 5–8) to find the difference:

The longer it took you to answer questions 5–8, the stronger the force of habit is in your life.

> **"Curious things, habits. People themselves never knew they had them."**
> —*Agatha Christie, mystery writer*

How habit-bound are you?
Rate yourself on a scale of 1–10, with 1 being very habit-bound.

10   5   1

Find Out MORE

✱ Choose a letter of the alphabet. For one week, change the way you write that letter. For example, if you usually write your a's this way,

a

try writing them this way:

a

Does trying to change a habit slow you down?

✱ Name three habits you have that make your life easier.

_____
_____
_____

✱ Name three habits you would like to change.

_____
_____
_____

> **"The victory of success is half won when one gains the habit of work."**
> —*Sarah Knowles Bolton, poet and social reformer*

PSI #19

ARE YOU SUGGESTIBLE?

Some people think for themselves. They won't take suggestions from anybody. Other people think whatever everybody else thinks. In between those two extremes are people who have their own ideas but are willing to take suggestions from others.

PART I: Read each question. Circle A, B, or C for the answer you would be most likely to choose.

1. You are absolutely sure you are supposed to meet your friend on Tuesday at 10 a.m., but a third friend thinks you are mistaken. What will you do?

   A. call your friend to verify your meeting time

   B. believe the third friend

   C. meet your friend at 10 a.m. on Tuesday without checking your calendar

2. Do you use slang words?

   A. sometimes

   B. often

   C. never

3. A vote is being taken by a show of hands. You are the only one who doesn't raise your hand to vote the way the others are voting. What will you do?

   A. not vote at all

   B. raise your hand and vote for what you don't want

   C. wait and vote the way you want to

4. If you think you know how to spell a word and three friends (all good spellers) tell you that you are wrong, what will you do?

   A. look up the word in a dictionary

   B. take their word for it

   C. don't change the word—leave it the way it is

5. You like your lunch box because you can put your thermos in it. But everyone else brings their lunch in a paper sack! What will you do?

   A. put your thermos in a sack, too

   B. stop bringing your thermos

   C. keep using your lunch box

PART II: The purpose of advertising is to suggest products to you so you will want to buy them. Ad writers know how suggestible most people are.

   You'll need a friend to help you do this part of the PSI. Ask the person to make two lists for you.

- List #1 should include 20 different current advertising slogans. These can be slogans for nationally advertised products, locally advertised products, services, TV shows, movies, political candidates, events—anything you are likely to see or hear in the media.

- List #2 should include the slogans plus the names of whatever they are advertising.

Ask your friends for List #1. Read through the slogans. How many can you identify?

WHAT'S YOUR STYLE?

PART I: Total your A's, B's, and C's.

A'S	B'S	C'S

- 3 or more A's mean you're somewhat suggestible.
- 3 or more B's mean you're very suggestible.
- 3 or more C's mean you do things your way, no matter what!

Find Out MORE

✱ Find out how suggestible your friends are. Ask them to take Parts I and II of this PSI, then compare your answers. (For Part II, you can create your own list of advertising slogans.)

✱ If you like guessing advertising slogans, play the Adverteasing game.

PART II: Check your answers against List #2.

- If you named 16 or more of the products, services, etc., you're very suggestible.
- If you named 12 or more, you're somewhat suggestible.
- If you guessed 9 or fewer, you're not very suggestible.

Being willing to take suggestions from others is a good quality. But there are times when it's best to follow your own ideas. Look at your scores from Parts I and II. How would you rate yourself?

> very suggestible
>
> somewhat suggestible
>
> not suggestible

Of course, there's another possibility: Maybe you just have a good memory.

ARE YOU A LEADER?

PSI #20

The best leaders are the ones in charge, right? Not always. People in power aren't necessarily good leaders. It takes the right attitudes to be a good leader—someone who motivates others to get things done.

Read questions 1–10. Circle A, B, or C for each one. Be as honest as you can!

1. You're working with a group to solve a problem. How do you feel when someone comes up with an idea that's obviously better than yours?

A. threatened

B. embarrassed

C. interested

2. You're working with a group on a project. How do you feel about your ideas compared to everyone else's ideas?

A. yours aren't as good

B. yours are better

C. yours are as good, but not necessarily better

3. What happens when you try to get "big ideas" across to other people?

A. they don't listen

B. they listen, but they don't "get it"

C. they usually listen and understand

4. You've been working on a project for a long time. So far, no one has given you any praise or feedback. What do you do?

A. get discouraged and quit

B. drop it and move on to a different idea

C. finish the project because you want to

5. You're invited to participate in a project—as a follower, not a leader. How do you feel about this?

A. good, because you're not comfortable leading anyway

B. you won't participate if you can't be the leader

C. you don't mind being a follower sometimes

6. What happens when you fail at something you try to do?

A. you quit because failing proves you're no good

B. you quit because others just don't realize how good you are

C. you try to learn something from the failure that will help you succeed in the future

7. If you were in charge of a group project, how would you handle it?

　A. let the others do most of the work

　B. do it all yourself to be sure it's done right

　C. break up the project into smaller parts, then assign them to people according to their skills and interests

8. How do you feel about working with people whose backgrounds are different from yours?

　A. uncomfortable about their differences

　B. superior or inferior to them

　C. interested in and respectful of their unique points of view

9. When someone gives you honest criticism, this makes you...

　A. hate yourself

　B. angry

　C. look for ways to improve

10. What do you do if you have a setback—if things don't go the way you want them to?

　A. dwell on your past mistakes and how things could have been

　B. blame other people for your setback

　C. look for positive ways to move forward

WHAT'S YOUR STYLE?
TOTAL YOUR A'S, B'S, AND C'S.

A'S	B'S	C'S

- **7 or more A's mean you may need more confidence in yourself before you can be a good leader.**

- **7 or more B's mean you may need more confidence in other people before you can be a good leader.**

- **7 or more C's mean you probably have a realistic view of yourself and other people. You have the right attitudes to be a good leader.**

If you scored lower than you hoped on leadership attitudes, try to figure out why. Do you lack confidence in yourself, or in other people? At some point in your life, you will probably be asked to lead. Working on good leadership attitudes can help you, even if you don't want to be the leader all the time.

Find Out MORE

✳ Ask your parents if you can lead a family outing—a picnic, a shopping trip, a ball game. Afterward, find out what your parents think of your leadership style.

✳ Who's your favorite leader? This can be a friend, a family member, someone in your community, even a world leader. What makes you look up to and admire this person? Write down a list of his or her qualities. Which of these qualities do you have?

"Ah well! I am their leader, I really ought to follow them."

—*Alexandre Auguste Ledru-Rolling, lawyer and politician*

WHAT BODY LANGUAGE DO YOU SPEAK?

Do you know that 55 percent of the messages you send to other people are sent with your body, not your words? The ways you sit, stand, and shake hands say things your words never do. In fact, only 7 percent of your messages are sent by words, and 38 percent are sent by your tone of voice.

For each question, circle the letter of the answer that's closest to your style.

1. HOW DO YOU SHAKE HANDS?

A. fingers only   B. your hand on top   C. using both of your hands   D. equal

2. WHICH IS YOUR NORMAL SITTING POSITION?

A. straddling chair   B. ankles crossed   C. leg over chair arm   D. legs crossed, hands behind head   E. leaning slightly forward, arms and legs relaxed

3. WHICH WAY DO YOU STAND MOST OFTEN?

A. hands on hips   B. arms folded   C. hands behind back   D. arms relaxed at your sides

4. WHICH IS YOUR USUAL WAY TO SIT AT YOUR SCHOOL DESK? (If you don't sit at a desk, then which is your usual way to sit at a table during a meeting or a discussion?)

A. leaning your head on your hand

B. fingers forming a steeple

C. leaning slightly forward, hands on desk or table

5. HOW OFTEN DURING A TYPICAL DAY DO YOU USE THESE GESTURES? MARK EACH WITH A NUMBER FROM 1 TO 5, WITH 1 BEING "ALMOST NEVER" AND 5 BEING "ALMOST ALWAYS."

A. rubbing your hands together _____

B. tapping your fingers _____

C. touching your face _____

D. crossing your arms _____

E. partially covering your eyes _____

WHAT'S YOUR STYLE?
HERE IS THE KEY TO INTERPRETING YOUR BODY LANGUAGE, ACCORDING TO BODY-LANGUAGE EXPERTS.

1. Shaking hands

A. "Don't get too friendly with me. I'm not sure I like you."

B. "I want to be in charge here!"

C. "Wow! I really want to be friends with you! You're just the most wonderful person I've ever met." (Hmmm! Does this sound a little insincere?)

D. "I feel fine about myself and fine about you. I'll be happy to be your friend if you'd like me to be."

2. Sitting

A. "I'm #1 here and this chair keeps you at an appropriate distance."

B. "I don't want to confide in anybody or let anybody know how I feel. I'm a little afraid."

C. "Who cares? I'm not interested in any of this."

D. "I'm definitely better than any of you, very confident about myself, and I feel open and relaxed right now."

E. "I'm willing to accept and treat you as an equal, if you do the same for me."

3. Standing

A. "I'm ready to take on this job, and I know I can handle it!" OR: "I'm not going to listen to anybody, especially someone in authority."

B. "I'm not sure I trust you. Stay out of my space."

C. "I'm in charge here."

D. "I feel relaxed and confident about myself."

4. Sitting at a desk or table

A. "I'm bored, and I'm not really paying attention."

B. "I'm pretty interested in what you're saying."

C. "I'm really interested in this. I'm willing to listen to your ideas and contribute some of my own."

• • • • • • • • • • • • • • • • •

5. Gestures

A. "I'm excited!"

B. "I'm bored."

C. "I feel self-conscious" OR "I have some doubts about this."

D. "NO! I'm going to resist whatever you say."

E. "Hurry up. I'm running out of patience."

"Emotion constantly finds expression in bodily position."
—Mabel Elsworth Todd, dancer, educator, and writer

SCORING: Give yourself 1 point for every time your body language communicates the message you mean to send. For example: Let's say your normal handshake is fingers-only. You want people to think you're standoffish. Give yourself 1 point. OR: Your normal handshake is fingers-only. But you want people to think you're friendly! Give yourself 0 points. When you're through scoring your body language, add up your points.

• **5 points mean that you always send the message you mean to send, and people always understand what you mean. Your body matches your words, and you're probably a good communicator.**

• **4 points mean that people almost always understand your message.**

• **3 points mean that people sometimes misunderstand your message. That sometimes causes problems.**

• **2 points mean that people often misunderstand your message. You have to explain yourself a lot.**

• **1 point means that people almost always misunderstand your message. You're constantly explaining what you really mean. Or you're constantly defending yourself, saying, "I didn't mean that!"**

Are you surprised by your score? Do you agree or disagree with what it says about your body language? If you agree, then you've just learned something about the silent messages you send. If you disagree, then maybe this PSI wasn't right for you. Maybe you have your own personal ways of shaking hands, sitting, standing, and so on that aren't at all like the ones in the pictures.

Whether you agree or disagree, you're still sending messages. Think about the messages you're sending. If your body is saying one thing and your words are saying another, you're wasting a lot of words!

Find Out MORE

✳ Play a game with your family, friends, or classmates. Decide on two opposite things to say—for example, "I think you're the most interesting person I've ever met" and "You put me to sleep." Say them in words. Then say them in body language. Now mix them up, putting "You're interesting" words with "You're boring" body language, and the other way around. How does this feel? What happens to your message when you mix it up?

✳ Change the way you normally sit in school or at the dinner table. Does anyone notice? Does your new position change the way your teachers or family react to you?

✳ Pick a pose you don't normally use—for example, the "superior" sitting position (illustration 2a). Try it for a few minutes. Do you start to feel superior?

✳ "Mirroring" is the technique of using the same body position and body language as someone you're with. It helps the other person feel more relaxed and comfortable. Salespeople and others often use mirroring to get others to agree with them. Try it sometime. What happens?

✳ Pay special attention to the body language of someone in the public eye—like a powerful leader, a popular entertainer, or a newscaster. Are there any unique gestures you might want to pick up on?

✳ Have you ever seen comedians impersonate famous people? They exaggerate the body language, gestures, and facial expressions of the people they impersonate. This is effective, funny, and fun! Play Personality Charades with a group of friends. Each player picks someone to impersonate (this can be a famous person, or any person known to everyone in the group). The rules are the same as for regular Charades. If you don't know how to play Charades, ask a parent or teacher to explain the game to you.

"Then you should say what you mean," the March Hare went on.

"I do," Alice hastily replied; "at least—at least I mean what I say—that's the same thing you know."

"Not the same thing a bit!" said the Hatter. "Why you might as well say that 'I see what I eat' is the same thing as 'I eat what I see'!"

—*Lewis Carroll*, Alice's Adventures in Wonderland

PSI #22

YOUR COMMUNICATION STYLE 1

Do you talk more like a "boss" or a "child"? Are you usually in "seeing mode" or "hearing mode"? The words you use reveal your communication style.

PART I: Circle A, B, or C for the statement in each group that sounds most like you.

1. A. *We should* go to the movie.
    B. *Let's* go to the movie.
    C. I *hope* we can go to the movie.

2. A. I *should* get help.
    B. I *will* get help.
    C. I *need* help.

3. A. I'd *better* hurry.
    B. I *will* hurry.
    C. I'll *try* to hurry.

4. A. We *must* eat now.
    B. We *can* eat now.
    C. We *need* to eat now.

5. A. We *should* win.
    B. We *could* win.
    C. We *need* to win.

6. A. You *never* remember my birthday.
    B. *Are* you going to remember my birthday?
    C. I *wish* you'd remember my birthday.

PART II: Circle A or B for the statement in each group that sounds most like you *right now*. For example, if someone came up to you and said, "I wish our teacher wouldn't assign so much home-work," how would you answer right now—"I hear what you're saying" or "I see what you're saying"?

1. A. I hear what you're saying.
    B. I see what you're saying.

2. A. Sounds interesting!
    B. I find that interesting!

3. A. It sounds like you're mad.
    B. I feel like you're mad.

4. A. I can tell you had a good time.
    B. It seems like you had a good time.

5. A. I understand that is true.
    B. I see that is true.

6. A. I can't get a handle on this problem.
    B. I can't find the answer to this problem.

7. A. Stop yelling, I don't want to hear another word!
    B. Stop yelling, I can't stand it!

8. A. See you around.
    B. Keep in touch.

9. A. Keep your ear to the ground.
    B. Keep your eye on the ball.

WHAT'S YOUR STYLE?

PART I: This part of the PSI tells you about your *ego states.* It is based on the work of psychologist Eric Berne, who believed that we sometimes live our lives by acting out "scripts" we learned when we were young. Dr. Berne identified three ego states: *parent, adult,* and *child.* Here is a chart of Dr. Berne's theory.

EGO STATES:

PARENT	ADULT	CHILD
Must	Will	Wish
Should	Can Do	Want
Ought	Is	Need
Better	Am	Hope
Never	Are	Try
Always		

- If you chose mostly A's, you're in a parent ego state. You see things in terms of "black and white." You may often feel like "the boss." Lucy, a character in the *Peanuts* comic strip, is often in a parent ego state.

- If you chose mostly B's, you're in an adult ego state. You feel in control without trying to control others. You just state the facts without much emotion.

- If you chose mostly C's, you're in a child ego state. You feel needy or helpless. You want other people to take charge so you can just have fun. The Three Stooges are examples of a child ego state.

You may change your ego state many times each day, depending on what you're doing, the people you're with, and the mood you're in.

TOTAL YOUR A'S, B'S, AND C'S:

| A'S | B'S | C'S |

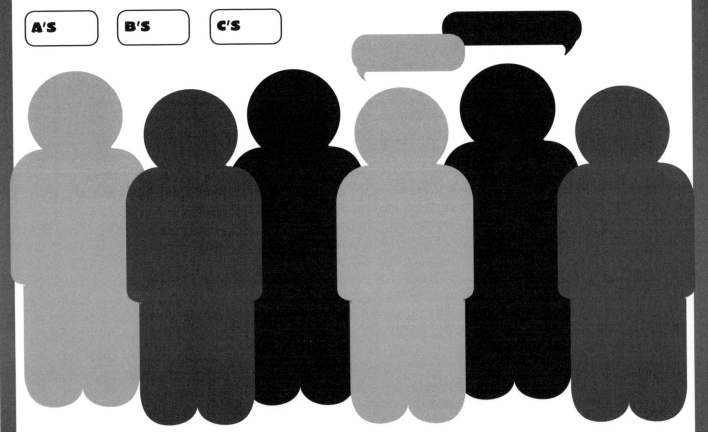

PART II: This part of the PSI tells you about your *sensory mode.* This has to do with which of your senses is usually strongest: *hearing, seeing,* or *feeling.*

For example, if you just finished a music lesson, you might be in a hearing mode. If you're thinking about your art project, you might be in a seeing mode. If you're hungry, you might be in a feeling mode.

This key will help you figure out what your answers mean.

Total your scores for each mode:

Hearing [ ]

Seeing [ ]

Feeling [ ]

A score of 6 or higher in any one mode means that you strongly favor it right now.

WHICH MODE DO YOU THINK YOU FAVOR MOST OFTEN?

1. A = hearing mode
   B = seeing mode

2. A = hearing mode
   B = seeing mode

3. A = hearing mode
   B = feeling mode

4. A = hearing mode
   B = feeling mode

5. A = feeling mode
   B = seeing mode

6. A = feeling mode
   B = seeing mode

7. A = hearing mode
   B = feeling mode

8. A = seeing mode
   B = feeling mode

9. A = hearing mode
   B = seeing mode

Find Out MORE

✱ Pay close attention to your communication style for a few days. Keep a diary of what you find out. Which ego state are you in most of the time? What about your sensory mode?

✱ Pay close attention to someone else's communication style for a few days. Choose a parent, a sister or brother, or a friend. What do you learn about that person's communication style?

✱ Is there anything about your communication style you'd like to change? Make a plan for changing it.

PSI #23

YOUR COMMUNICATION STYLE 2

Does your self-talk help you or hurt you? How persuasive are you? Learn more about your communication style.

PART I: Circle A or B for the one that sounds most like the way you would talk to yourself or think about yourself.

1. You're breathing rapidly and trembling a little. What do you say to yourself?

   A. "I'm really nervous!"

   B. "I'm really excited!"

2. You're facing a challenge. What do you tell yourself?

   A. "I'll try to do it."

   B. "I'll do it!"

3. There's something you know you shouldn't do. How do you tell yourself?

   A. "I can't do this!"

   B. "I won't do this!"

4. There's something you need to do. What do you say to yourself?

   A. "I should get this done."

   B. "I could get this done."

5. Today everything went wrong! What do you tell yourself?

   A. "I really messed up today."

   B. "This just wasn't my day."

6. You tried out for something (a position on a team, student government, the lead in a play) and didn't get it. What do you say to yourself?

   A. "I'm a loser."

   B. "It just didn't work out."

7. You entered a contest based on a skill (chess, swimming, gymnastics, spelling bee) and didn't win, even though you did your best. What do you tell yourself?

   A. "If only I'd done better!"

   B. "This just wasn't my time."

PART II: Circle A or B for the one that sounds most like what you would say.

1. You're trying to get your brother to pay back some money he borrowed. You ask him...

   A. "Are you going to pay me back?"

   B. "When are you going to pay me back?"

2. You'd like to earn extra credit in math class. You ask your teacher...

   A. "Is there any way to get extra credit in this class?"

   B. "How can I earn extra credit in this class?"

3. You want your sister to help with the dishes. You ask her...

   A. "Will you help me with the dishes?"

   B. "Would you rather rinse the dishes or load the dishwasher?"

4. You need an increase in your allowance. You ask your parents...

   A. "Can I have a raise in my allowance?"

   B. "Since I have more responsibility now, when will my allowance be raised?"

5. You'd like your dad to play checkers with you. You say to him...

 A. "I know you're really busy, but...will you play checkers with me?"

 B. "How about we play some checkers after dinner?"

6. There's a new movie playing, and you want your whole family to go. You announce...

 A. "Let's all go to a movie!"

 B. "I'll do the dishes, and then we can all go to a movie."

WHAT'S YOUR STYLE?

PART I: This part of the PSI tells you about your self-talk. Your self-talk is closely related to your personal power. Positive self-talk adds to your personal power. Negative self-talk takes away from your personal power.

TOTAL YOUR A'S AND B'S:

A'S	B'S

- **5 or more A's mean that you use a lot of negative self-talk.**

- **5 or more B's means that you use a lot of positive self-talk.**

The more positive self-talk you use, the greater your personal power, and the more control you have over your life.

PART II: This part of the PSI tells you how persuasive you are.

TOTAL YOUR A'S AND B'S:

A'S	B'S

- **4 or more B's mean that you're very persuasive. It's fairly easy for you to get other people to do what you'd like them to do.**

- **4 or more A's mean that you're not very persuasive. You might have a hard time getting people to cooperate with you.**

Find Out MORE

✷ Pay close attention to your communication style for a few days. Keep a diary of what you find out. Do you use more positive or negative self-talk? Are you a persuasive person?

✷ Pay close attention to someone else's communication style for a few days. Choose a parent, a brother or sister, or a friend. What do you learn about that person's communication style?

PSI #24

ARE YOU RIGHT-BRAINED OR LEFT-BRAINED?

Did you know that your brain is made up of two halves? The *left* side of your brain controls the *right* side of your body, and the *right* side of your brain controls the *left* side of your body. The two halves are connected by a system of fibers called the *corpus callosum.*

In 1940, some doctors cut the corpus callosum of patients with epilepsy. They wanted to see if this would "trap" the patients' seizures on one side of the brain so the other side could function normally. It seemed to work.

In 1960, a scientist named Roger Sperry studied patients who had been through this operation. He noticed some interesting things about them. His "split-brained" patients could hold an object in their right hand and name it. But when

they held an object in their left hand, they could describe it, but they couldn't name it! Sperry also found that these patients could write with their right hands but not draw. They could draw with their left hands but not write.

Sperry's studies seemed to show that each half of the brain has different characteristics and abilities. The left half is logical, analytical, and used for verbal tasks. The right half sees things "whole" instead of in parts, and is used for creative thinking.

Now people talk about being "left-brained" (logical) or "right-brained" (creative). But brain science is really much more complicated than that. The latest thinking and research puts the focus on being "whole-brained." Still, thinking about how our brains function can tell us more about our personal style.

Read each question, then circle A or B for the answer that you would most likely choose.

1. Which is more true of you?
   A. I am tense about getting things right
   B. I am relaxed and let things happen

2. Do you often feel sad or down in the dumps?
   A. no
   B. yes

3. Which do you enjoy more about music?
   A. the beat
   B. the melody

4. Which way of learning do you like best?
   A. books and lectures
   B. workshops and field trips

5. Which of these two subjects do you like more?
   A. math
   B. art

6. Which of these two games do you prefer?
   A. Scrabble
   B. checkers

7. How do you usually buy something?
   A. I think about its value and how I will use it
   B. I just buy it

8. When you buy something, do you make sure to get the correct change back?
   A. yes, I count it
   B. no

9. How do you figure things out?
   A. a piece at a time, then put it all together
   B. the answer comes to me all at once, like a light going on

10. Which of these two types of puzzles do you prefer?
    A. crossword puzzles
    B. jigsaw puzzles

11. How often do you have a hunch?
    A. never or almost never
    B. often

12. Which would you rather do?
    A. read
    B. watch TV

13. How are you at putting your feelings into words?
    A. very good
    B. it is hard for me

14. If you practice an instrument or a sport, how do you do it?
    A. the same time each day, for a certain amount of time
    B. when I feel like it and have the time

15. You're riding your bike to a friend's house. You've never been there before. Which method do you use to find your way?
    A. I ask for directions, then write down street names and landmarks
    B. I ask for the address, then look at a map

16. Which of these types of fabrics do you prefer?
    A. fabrics without much texture (cotton, denim)
    B. fabrics with lots of texture (corduroy, suede, velvet)

17. Are you good at remembering faces?
    A. no
    B. yes

18. Are you good at remembering names?
    A. yes
    B. no

19. How do you feel about psychic claims—that there is such a thing as ESP, for example?
    A. they are foolish and nonscientific
    B. science can't explain everything; they are worth looking into

20. Are you a better athlete than you are a student?
    A. no
    B. yes

WHAT'S YOUR STYLE?

TOTAL YOUR A'S AND B'S.

A's are left-brained responses; B's are right-brained responses.

A'S	B'S

- 17 or more A's or B's mean you have a strong preference for that side of your brain.

- 15 A's or B's mean you have some preference for that side of your brain.

- 10 or 11 of each mean you use both sides of your brain equally.

If you're right-brained, does that mean you're never logical? If you're left-brained, does that mean you're never creative? Of course not. All it means is that you tend to favor one side over the other. It's just part of your personal style.

Find Out MORE

✱ Test your family members and friends. Are they left-brained or right-brained?

✱ Which hand do you normally use for writing? Stick that hand in your pocket and keep it there for 15 minutes or so. Meanwhile, try doing simple tasks with your other hand—changing TV channels, dialing the phone, opening a door, zipping a zipper. Is this easy or hard for you to do?

> "You are old, Father William," the young man said,
> "And your hair has become very white;
> And yet you incessantly stand on your head—
> Do you think, at your age, it is right?"
> "In my youth," Father William replied to his son,
> "I feared it might injure the brain;
> But now that I'm perfectly sure I have none,
> Why, I do it again and again."
>
> —*Lewis Carroll,* Alice's Adventures in Wonderland

WHICH SIDE IS IN CONTROL?

Which side of your brain controls most of your activities? Find out with this simple exercise. Remember that the left side of your brain controls the right side of your body, and the right side of your brain controls the left side of your body.

1. Clasp your hands together. Which thumb is on top? _____

2. Fold your arms. Which arm is on top? _____

3. Cross your legs. Which leg is on top? _____

4. Look through a paper tube. Which eye do you use? _____

5. Kick a ball. Which foot do you use? _____

Which side of your brain is in control? _____

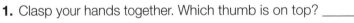

HOW INVENTIVE ARE YOU?

PSI #25

In PSI #24, you learned that the right side of your brain is creative and the left side is logical. You learned which side of your brain is stronger. What if you're left-brained? Does this mean that you aren't (or can't be) creative? Not at all. Many people believe that you can train the right side of your brain to take over at times. It's also possible for your right brain to take over all by itself. Most people are already more creative than they realize!

Inventiveness is a special form of creativity. Some people think of it as creativity's "practical side," because to invent something is to create something that solves a problem or satisfies a human want or need. One of the greatest artists of all time, Leonardo da Vinci, was also one of the greatest inventors.

As you find out how inventive you are, you'll learn how much you already use your right brain without needing to work on it.

Answer each question Yes or No.

1. Have you ever solved a problem?

Yes   No

2. Have you ever made up a joke?

Yes   No

3. Have you ever made up a riddle?

Yes   No

4. Have you ever created an original drawing, cartoon, or song?

Yes   No

5. Have you ever made up a story? (It doesn't matter whether you wrote it down or not.)

Yes   No

6. Have you ever made up a game, or changed the rules of a game?

Yes   No

7. Have you ever added a special ingredient to your food that most other people don't use?

Yes   No

8. Have you ever made do with something because you didn't have the proper equipment? (For example: pounding in a nail with a shoe.)

Yes   No

WHAT'S YOUR STYLE?

If you answered Yes even once, then you are indeed inventive! Actually, most people could answer Yes to all or most of these questions. The point is, we're all more inventive than we think we are.

> "Creativity requires the courage to let go of certainty."
> —Erich Fromm, psychologist

Find Out MORE

✽ Most children invent words of their own when they are first learning the language. These are often very descriptive—and very funny! Ask your parents if you ever made any of these "word inventions."

✽ If you can, spend some time around a toddler. Pay attention to the many inventions she or he comes up with, both in action and in language.

✽ Every time you find a better or faster way to do something, you are thinking like an inventor. You can apply this thinking process to housework, yard work, homework, or party-giving. Plan the most efficient way you can think of to do one of your daily chores or routines, or combine several into one. Become an efficiency expert for a week.

ATTENTION INVENTORS!

You say you've invented a toilet-lid lock? An eyeglass frame with adjustable rearview mirrors? A carry-all hat with a top that acts like a purse? A baby-patting machine? An electronic snore depressor?

Too bad; you're not the first. All of these inventions have already been patented.

But maybe there's something else in your head or on your drawing board. Something that really is your own invention.

In the United States, the right to patent inventions is guaranteed by the Constitution of the United States, Article I, Section 8, which reads, "The Congress shall have Power...to promote the Progress of Science and useful Arts, by securing for limited Times to...Inventors the exclusive Right to their respective...Discoveries."

To be patentable, an invention must be *useful,* and it must also be new. You must be able to explain, in writing and sometimes in drawings, what makes your invention unique. You must also pay a filing fee.

If you want to learn more about patents and patenting, write or call: Patent and Trademark Office, PO Box 1450, Alexandria, VA 22313; telephone 1-800-786-9199. Or visit them online (www.uspto.gov).

WHAT'S YOUR C.Q.?

You've probably heard of I.Q., which stands for "Intelligence Quotient" and is supposed to be a measure of how smart you are. C.Q. stands for "Creativity Quotient." Check yours with this revealing PSI.

Give yourself anywhere from 1–10 points for each of the 10 creativity characteristics listed below.

- 10 points = you're very much the way the question describes
- 9, 8, 7, or 6 points = you're pretty much that way
- 5 points = you're average for that characteristic
- 4, 3, or 2 points = you're lower than average for that characteristic
- 1 point = you aren't that way at all

Highest possible score: 100 points
Lowest possible score: 10 points

1. **Are you a curious cat?** Do you wonder why, how, why not? Do you enjoy collecting bits of information? Do you ask questions? Do you question the obvious?

2. **Are you observant?** Did you notice when the house down the street was painted? When the market got a new sign? When your aunt got a new hairdo? When the newspaper changed its column width?

3. **Do you see other points of view?** When you disagree with people, are you able to understand their side? Can you see new ways of looking at old problems?

4. **Are you willing to change your ideas?** Are you open to new ideas? If someone can add to your idea and improve it, will you change it? Do you search for the best idea rather than stick to your idea?

5. **Can you learn from your mistakes and move on?** Do you accept failure without just giving up? Do you realize that if you don't give up, then you haven't really failed?

6. **Do you use your imagination and dreams?** Do you say "What if ...?"

7. **Do you see connections between things that seem unrelated?** (For example, do a desert plant and a tough person have anything in common?) Do you re-combine ideas in new ways (like using a glass for a flower vase)?

8. **Do you believe in yourself?** Do you have a can-do attitude? Do you expect to find solutions to problems?

9. **Do you try to keep from judging other people, ideas, and situations?** Do you wait until all the evidence is in before making up your mind?

10. **Do you have a fun attitude?** Will you do things even if they look silly? Do you trust yourself enough to be adventurous and take risks? Will you suggest a solution that might be rejected by others, or do you usually play it safe?

WHAT'S YOUR STYLE?

TOTAL YOUR SCORE TO FIND YOUR CREATIVITY QUOTIENT.

- **80–100 points = you're a Creativity Genius**

- **60–80 points = you're more creative than most people**

- **40–60 points = you're about as creative as most people**

- **20–40 points = you're less creative than most people**

- **10–20 points = you could use some creativity classes!**

"Odd how the creative power at once brings the whole universe to order."

—*Virginia Woolf, writer and literary critic*

Find Out MORE

✻ If you scored 20 points or below, maybe it's time to put yourself on a Creativity Curriculum. Try an art class. Or, when you get up each morning, notice something new about the day, yourself, or what you see out the window. Or come up with your own idea:

_____

_____

_____

_____

_____

_____

_____

_____

_____

_____

✻ If you scored between 20 and 60, try to find ways to become more creative. (Isn't it about time to redecorate your room?)

✻ If you scored 60 or above, let your creativity show! Pursue hobbies you enjoy. Learn to paint, draw, use a camera, carve wood. These activities will bring you happiness for the rest of your life.

PSI #27

TEST YOUR CREATIVITY

Creativity is a mysterious trait. Experts keep coming up with different ways to define and measure it. Dr. E. Paul Torrance, an expert in creativity, has broken down the creative thinking process into these four characteristics:

1. *fluency* (how many ideas you can come up with)

2. *flexibility* (how many different kinds of ideas you can come up with)

3. *originality* (are your ideas your own, or borrowed?)

4. *elaboration* (how detailed your ideas are)

You can use these four characteristics to find out how creative you are. You may surprise yourself!

Look closely at each of these shapes. What do you think they are? What do you think they might be? Come up with as many ideas as you can. Be brave—be crazy! There are no right or wrong answers. Give yourself five minutes. Ready? Set? GO!

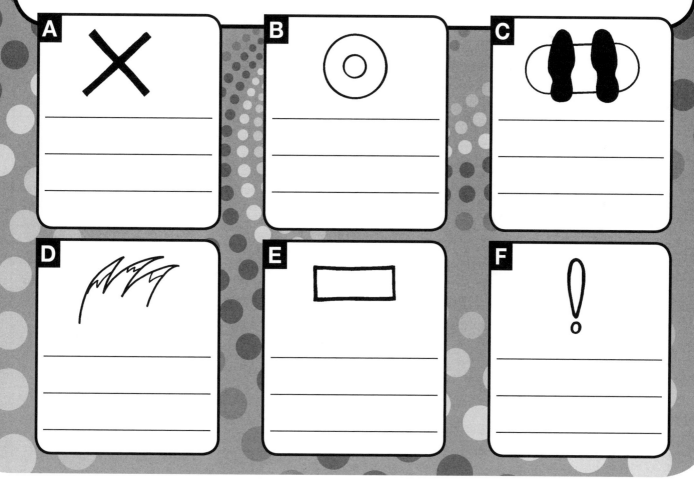

A

_____
_____
_____

B

_____
_____
_____

C

_____
_____
_____

D

_____
_____
_____
_____

E

_____
_____
_____

F

_____
_____
_____

WHAT'S YOUR STYLE?

1. **How many ideas did you come up with for each shape?**

A: _____   B: _____   C: _____

D: _____   E: _____   F: _____

Total your points to get your *fluency* score: [ ]

2. **How many different kinds of ideas did you come up with? TIP: Think of each kind as a "category." A category might be "clothes," "food," "animals," or "furniture." For example, if you wrote "cowboy hat" and "sombrero" for shape B, give yourself 1 point because both are in the same category. If you wrote "cowboy hat," "donut," "snake," and "pillow," give yourself 4 points.**

A: _____   B: _____   C: _____

D: _____   E: _____   F: _____

Total your points to get your *flexibility* score: [ ]

3. **How many original ideas did you come up with? If you did this PSI in a group, compare ideas and cross out any that appear on more than one person's list. If you did this PSI on your own, compare your ideas with the ones listed here. Cross out anything you wrote that's the same or very similar.**

   A. the 24th letter of the alphabet, a cross, 2 sticks

   B. a donut, a wheel, a ring, a lifesaver

   C. two splotches, muddy footprints, inkblots

   D. ocean waves, flames

   E. a square, a box, a sign, a hole in the ground, a refrigerator

   F. an exclamation point, a bat and ball, a tube squeezing out toothpaste

Give yourself 1 point for every original idea you had:

A: _____   B: _____   C: _____

D: _____   E: _____   F: _____

Now total your points to get your *originality* score: [ ]

4. **How detailed are the ideas you came up with? Give yourself 1 point for each adjective you used, 1 point for each adverb, and 1 point for each verb (action word). For example, "Sombrero on table" would get no points. "Sombrero sitting on table" would get one point (for "sitting"). "Straw sombrero balancing on head of old man riding a bicycle" would get four points (for "straw," "balancing," "old," and "riding").**

A: _____   B: _____   C: _____

D: _____   E: _____   F: _____

Total your points to get your *elaboration* score: [ ]

Now add up your scores to find your Grand Total:

Fluency score: _____

Flexibility score: _____

Originality score: _____

Elaboration score: _____

GRAND TOTAL CREATIVITY SCORE: [ ]

If you did this PSI in a group, you can compare your scores. What does this tell you about your creativity? If you did this PSI on your own, give yourself a Creativity Rating. On a scale of 1–10, with 1 being NOT very creative, how creative are you?

10 ——————— 5 ——————— 1

> "A ship in port is safe, but that's not what ships are built for."
>
> —Grace Hopper, inventor

WHAT OTHER CREATIVE PEOPLE SAW

I have given this Creativity Test to young people in classes and workshops. Here are some of the more creative ideas they came up with. How do yours compare?

A. a tepee, two stick people

B. a germ's view of a microscope, a lady with a big hat at the beach

C. a man standing on his head, a keyhole in a glass door

D. a porcupine in the wind, close-up of a spiral notebook

E. a graduate, view of thick fog out a window

F. a bottle dumping out one last drop, a clown looking up and saying "oh"

Find Out MORE

✱ Now that you've taken the Creativity Test, found out your score, and read about things that other people saw, you may want to take the test again. See if you score higher this time.

✱ Try "creating" something. Use materials you have at hand or can find easily. Make something useful, or something beautiful. You'll be amazed at what you can make out of nearly nothing.

✱ Read about other creative people. Ask your teacher or librarian to help you find some interesting biographies.

TIME OUT THE MMPI—A FAMOUS PERSONALITY TEST

One of the most famous and popular personality tests is the **M**innesota **M**ultiphasic **P**ersonality **I**nventory, or MMPI for short. Psychologists use it to find out more about the people who come to see them. Many employers use it to screen people who are applying for jobs.

The MMPI is made up of 550 first-person statements. These statements are about habits, preferences, fears, attitudes, relationships, behaviors, and beliefs. After reading each statement, the test-taker responds "true," "false," or "cannot say."

The test and its statements are a big secret. Only licensed psychologists can get copies. You will never find large parts of the MMPI printed in popular books or magazines.

Many people have complaints about the MMPI. They think it's too old (it was created in 1940). They think the statements are too old-fashioned. They even think the test is sexist and racist, or slanted in favor of people who are religious. But psychologists keep giving it anyway.

One reason the MMPI is so popular is because it's supposed to be cheat-proof. If you try to cheat on the test to make yourself look good, the people who score the test will be able to tell.

It's funny, but people cheat on personality tests all the time. They try to create a picture of themselves that might not be true. It's better to be honest when you answer questions about your personality. Honest answers will help you learn more about your personal style.

ARE YOU A REAL GENIUS?

What does it mean to be a genius? What are geniuses really like? John Briggs, author of *Fire in the Crucible: The Alchemy of Creative Genius* (New York: St. Martin's Press, 1988), studied geniuses to find out if they have anything in common. This is what he discovered:

- Geniuses are both humble and conceited.
- They feel an intense need to work hard.
- They concentrate to the point of obsession.
- They see the world differently than most people do.
- They explore new possibilities.

Briggs concluded that geniuses are not necessarily smarter than non-geniuses. They just notice details that other people overlook. They have a different vision of what is important in the world. They have certain *attitudes.* For example: They are open-minded; they learn from mistakes; they care about the world.

This quiz measures your attitudes. Try to take it at the end of the day.
Ask yourself these 12 questions to see if you've been a genius today. Check Yes or No for each.

1. Have you looked at old information in a brand new way?

   Yes   No

2. Have you made new connections in different content areas (like seeing the "math" in art or the "music" in math)?

   Yes   No

3. Have you wondered whether you were really smart?

   Yes   No

4. Have you learned one new thing about yourself?

   Yes   No

5. Have you learned one new thing about the world?

   Yes   No

6. Have you learned one new thing about other people or another person?

   Yes   No

7. Have you learned from at least one mistake?

   Yes   No

8. Have you pursued your goals, even if you felt you were failing?

   Yes   No

9. Have you felt that you had to be the one who "knows it all"?

   Yes   No

10. Have your opinions been the same as most people's?

    Yes   No

11. Have you recognized and made use of other people's skills and strengths?

    Yes   No

12. Have you had an original idea, shared it with other people, and accepted honest criticism?

    Yes   No

WHAT'S YOUR STYLE?

USE THIS KEY TO FIGURE OUT YOUR SCORE.

Question	Points for your answer	
#	YES	NO
1.	10	0
2.	10	0
3.	0	10
4.	5	0
5.	2	0
6.	3	0
7.	10	0
8.	10	0
9.	0	10
10.	0	5
11.	10	0
12.	15	0

BONUS: Give yourself 5 points if you've done something you love to do. This can be almost anything—gardening, listening to music, cooking, writing a poem, whatever.

Total your points: ____

- 60 or more points = you've been a real genius today!
- 50–60 points = you've got real genius potential
- 40–50 points = you're looking at the world the way most people do
- 40 or fewer points = try harder tomorrow to open your mind!

"One is not born a genius, one becomes a genius."
—Simone de Beauvoir, writer and philosopher

Find Out MORE

* Read about geniuses like physicist Albert Einstein, writer Virginia Woolf, sculptor Louise Nevelson, and composer Wolfgang Amadeus Mozart. Ask your teacher or librarian for help in finding books or articles about them (or other geniuses). Do you have anything in common with them? Are there ways in which you'd like to be like them?

* If you don't think you're a genius, don't worry about it. Most people in the world aren't geniuses, and they still invent things, have careers, write books, and enjoy their lives. Some geniuses are never recognized as geniuses during their lifetimes. What's important is to be open to new ideas, and practice looking at things in new ways. These are the characteristics that matter the most.

DOES IT TAKE A REAL GENIUS TO BECOME PRESIDENT OF THE UNITED STATES?

Some people measure genius by how educated someone is. In fact, nine Presidents of the United States never went to college. Can you name them? The answers are printed upside down below.

_____

_____

_____

_____

_____

_____

_____

_____

_____

> "Neither a lofty degree of intelligence nor imagination nor both together go to the making of genius. Love, love, love, that is the soul of genius."
>
> —*Wolfgang Amadeus Mozart, composer*

George Washington, Andrew Jackson, Martin Van Buren, Zachary Taylor, Millard Fillmore, Abraham Lincoln, Andrew Johnson, Grover Cleveland, Harry Truman

PSI #29

WHO'S SMART?

PART I: Pick the person in each group you think is most intelligent.

GROUP A

___ Kevin Garnett, athlete

___ Justin Timberlake, singer

___ Halle Berry, actress and Oscar winner

___ Sally Ride, astronaut

GROUP B

___ Sarah Hughes, Olympic athlete

___ Alicia Keys, singer

___ Brad Pitt, actor

___ Donald J. Cram, scientist and Nobel Prize winner

GROUP C

___ Charles Schulz, creator of the *Peanuts* cartoon characters

___ Bishop Desmond Tutu, Nobel Peace Prize winner

___ Gary Kasparov, chess champion

___ Mother Teresa of Calcutta, Nobel Peace Prize winner

Was it hard to choose? If yes, then you're smart. Because each of these individuals is intelligent in different ways.

Like creativity, intelligence is difficult to define and measure. Experts keep coming up with different ways to think about it. Psychologist Howard Gardner studied intelligence for a long time. He finally decided that there are seven different kinds of intelligence. He gave each one a name and identified the kinds of people most likely to have it:

1. **Bodily-Kinesthetic Intelligence** (athletes, surgeons, inventors)
2. **Spatial Intelligence** (chess players, architects, map makers)
3. **Logical-Mathematical Intelligence** (scientists, mathematicians, logicians)
4. **Musical Intelligence** (composers, conductors, performers)
5. **Linguistic Intelligence** (authors, journalists, editors)
6. **Interpersonal Intelligence** (diplomats, religious leaders, political leaders)
7. **Intrapersonal Intelligence** (psychologists, counselors)

In other words, "being smart" means much more than getting straight A's in school!

Think about all the things you can do. Think about the things you're especially good at. What kinds of intelligence do you have?

PART II: Fill in the blanks with the names of people you know. If you can't think of someone who's right for a blank, then fill it in with the name of a famous person.

1. If I ever get lost, I hope I'm with _____ .

2. If I ever own a basketball team, I want _____ to be a player.

3. If I move to a new place and need to learn my way around, I hope I can be with _____ .

4. If I enter a poster contest, I want _____ on my team.

5. When my radio breaks, I hope _____ will be home so I can call for help.

6. For my Trivial Pursuit game partner, I want _____ .

7. For my tennis partner, I want _____ .

8. If I work on an invention, I want _____ to help me.

9. I definitely want to have _____ on my debate team.

10. If I start a musical group and need to find musicians, I sure hope I can get _____ to join.

10. For a fun time at a party, I always invite _____ .

10. When I need advice about a problem, I will always call on _____ .

10. We're going to try to get the school cafeteria to change its menu. I hope _____ will be our leader when we do this.

WHAT'S YOUR STYLE?

All of the people you named above have special kinds of intelligence. Humor, sense of direction, athletic ability, memory, music, art, problem solving, social sense, and leadership are all intelligences. So you were smart to pick those people!

What are your special intelligences?

> "The Artist is not a different kind of person, but every person is a different kind of artist."
>
> —*Eric Gill, philosopher*

Find Out MORE

✳ Share this PSI with a friend. Ask him or her to complete Part II. Which blanks do you hope your name ends up in?

✳ Is there an intelligence you wish you had more of? What can you do to get smarter?

PSI #30

ARE YOU A CRITICAL THINKER?

A critical thinker is someone who doesn't accept the first answer that pops into her or his head. A critical thinker says, "Wait a minute. Does this seem logical and reasonable? Is a better answer possible?" This PSI helps you find out if you're a critical thinker. It's also full of fun brain teasers. Answer these questions. But watch out—some of them are tricky!

PART I: PROBLEM SOLVING

1. There are 64 checkers players at a tournament. A player is eliminated when he or she loses a game. How many games must the champion play?

2. The electricity goes out, and your bedroom is pitch dark. Yet you still need to find a matching pair of socks! In your drawer are 25 white socks and 25 red socks. How many socks must you take out of the drawer before you get a matching pair?

3. If you have two U.S. coins totaling 55 cents and one of the coins is not a nickel, what are the two coins?

4. If three cats kill three rats in three minutes, how long will it take for 100 cats to kill 100 rats?

5. A farmer had 17 chickens. All but 9 died. How many does the farmer have left?

6. Is it legal in Canada for a man to marry his widow's sister?

1. Change this line so that no empty glass is next to another empty glass, and no full glass is next to another full glass. You may touch and move only one glass.

Explain how you did this:

_____

_____

_____

8. Three men are walking in the rain with no umbrellas and no hats. Two get their hair wet and one doesn't. Why?

9. A girl went door-to-door selling eggs. At the first house, she sold half her eggs plus half an egg. At the second house, she sold half her eggs plus half an egg. At the third house, she sold half her eggs plus half an egg. After this, she had no eggs left—she had sold all her eggs. How many did she start with?

10. You have a 9-gallon container and a 4-gallon container. How can you measure out exactly 6 gallons of water from a tank without using any other container?

PART II: TRUE OR FALSE?

Circle T for true, F for false, and give a reason for your answer.

1. If penicillin cures an infection, then the lack of penicillin in the bloodstream must cause the infection.

T   F _____

_____

2. Tim and Tom play the lottery. Tim picks numbers 9, 17, 22, 48, 6, and 10. Tom picks numbers 9, 10, 11, 12, 13, and 14. Tim has a better chance of winning than Tom.

T   F _____

_____

3. Since nobody seems to be able to prove that Santa Claus does not exist, it's reasonable to assume that he likely does exist.

T   F _____

_____

4. If statistics show that ice cream sales go up with the number of hours infants spend fussing, this means that fussy infants cause people to go out and buy ice cream.

T   F _____

_____

5. If a study shows that children who spend their preschool years in a childcare center are more likely to finish college than children who are cared for at home, we can assume that childcare centers educate children better than parents at home.

T   F _____

_____

PART III: MULTIPLE CHOICE

Circle the letter of your answer.

1. A penny doubled every day would give you, at the end of 30 days,

   a. $3.00

   b. $18.00

   c. $250.00

   d. $10,000,000

2. How many times will you need to shuffle a deck of cards to make sure the deck is mixed up?

   a. 1 time

   b. 2–3 times

   c. 6–8 times

3. Two people are picked at random from the population of the United States. What are the chances that Person One will know someone who knows someone who knows Person Two?

   a. almost certain (99/100)

   b. very unlikely (1/100)

   c. even (50/50)

4. Four people are meeting for the first time. Two of them have the same astrological sign. How do you feel about this?

   a. amazed

   b. unimpressed (this is expected)

   c. confused

5. You want to buy a new computer. In January, it goes on sale for 40% off. But you still can't afford it. Then, in March, it's reduced by 40% more! You go to buy it, knowing you'll save this much off the original price:

   a. 80%

   b. 64%

   c. 75%

WHAT'S YOUR STYLE?
HERE ARE THE ANSWERS TO EACH QUESTION.

PART I: PROBLEM SOLVING

1. six (64 players ÷ 2 players per game = 32 players left ÷ 2 = 16 ÷ 2 = 8 ÷ 2 = 4 ÷ 2 = 2, CHAMPIONSHIP GAME)

2. three (think about it!)

3. a 50 cent piece and a nickel (one is a nickel—but one is not a nickel)

4. three minutes (more cats and more rats don't equal more time)

5. nine (read the question again—and this time, pay attention!)

6. no (he's dead)

7. Pick up glass #2 and pour it into glass #5. Then set #2 back in place.

8. the third man is bald

9. seven (FIRST HOUSE: half of 7 = 3½, + ½ egg = 4 eggs sold, 3 remaining; SECOND HOUSE: half of 3 = 1½, + ½ egg = 2 eggs sold, 1 remaining; THIRD HOUSE: half of 1 = ½, + ½ egg = 1 egg sold, 0 remaining)

10. Turn the 4-gallon container into a container that will measure out 3 gallons by filling it with one gallon of water. You can get one gallon of water by filling the 9-gallon container and emptying 4 gallons into the 4-gallon container. Now the 9-gallon container has 5 gallons in it (9 - 4 = 5). Empty the 4-gallon container and fill it again from the 9-gallon container. Now the 9-gallon container has 1 gallon (5 - 4 = 1). Empty the 4-gallon container again and put the 1 gallon of water in it. Now it will take 3 gallons of water to fill the 4-gallon container. Fill the 9-gallon container and dump enough water from it to fill the 4-gallon container the rest of the way. Nine gallons minus 3 gallons leaves 6 gallons in the 9-gallon container!

SCORING: Correct answers to questions 1–8 are worth 3 points each. The correct answer to question 9 is worth 10 points; the correct answer to question 10 is worth 15 points. Total points possible: 50.

YOUR SCORE:

PART II: TRUE OR FALSE?

1. *False.* You can't assume that the reverse of something is true. Although this works in some cases (sleep cures tiredness, lack of sleep causes tiredness), obviously we can't say things like, "Since aspirin relieves headaches, lack of aspirin must cause headaches."

2. *False.* When choosing six numbers out of 40 chances for a lottery, any combination is as likely to come up as any other combination. Just because the numbers are in sequence doesn't decrease their likelihood of coming up.

3. *False.* Disproving the existence of something is very difficult. But just because you can't disprove the existence of something doesn't mean its existence is therefore proven! Maybe this fact of logic is why our legal system says that a person is innocent until proven guilty. When charged with a crime, you don't have to prove that you didn't do it. Rather, it must be proved that you *did* do it.

4. *False.* Fussy babies and ice cream sales are both caused by 100° temperatures and uncomfortable weather conditions.

5. *False.* This information actually tells us nothing—or, rather, we can't say what it does tell us. It may be that child care facilities are teaching children more, or it may be that children in childcare have two working parents who can afford to send them to college in later years. Too often, a little information is interpreted to mean a lot more than it does!

SCORING: Give yourself 5 points for each correct answer. Total points possible: 25.

YOUR SCORE:

PART III: MULTIPLE CHOICE

1. The answer is d. To be exact, you'd have $10,737,418.24! So who said pennies were worthless?

2. The answer is c. If you shuffle only a couple of times, a magician who knows the original order of the deck will usually be able to find a card that you remove and replace. (Much of what looks like "magic" is just skillful entertainment.)

3. The answer is a. The chances are almost certain.

4. The answer is b. At least two will have the same sign four times out of ten.

5. The answer is b. First you save 40%, which leaves 60%. Then you save 40% of the remaining 60%, or 24%. 40% + 24% = 64%.

SCORING: Give yourself 5 points for each correct answer. Total points possible: 25.

YOUR SCORE:

ADD UP YOUR SCORES FROM ALL THREE PARTS. THERE ARE 100 POSSIBLE POINTS IN ALL.

- 75–100 points = you're an excellent critical thinker

- 50–75 points = you're a pretty good critical thinker

- 25–50 points = your critical thinking skills could use some sharpening

- 0–25 points = try again!

Find Out MORE

✱ If you scored low on these questions, ask your teachers and parents to help you become a better critical thinker. There are many books and exercises that can help develop critical thinking skills.

✱ Whether you did well or not so well, look back at the questions and think about why you answered them the way you did. What thoughts led to your answers? Did a skill you already have—like multiplication or algebra—help you solve one or more problems?

✱ If you enjoyed these brain teasers, be sure to see Read More About It on page 125.

PSI #31

HOW'S YOUR MEMORY?

How do you remember things? Do they just stick to your memory without any effort from you? Or do you have a special system—something you do to make sense out of things so you can remember them later? (Like turning them into songs, relating them to the ABCs, or creating rhymes?) Another term for memory system is *mnemonic device.* Examples of mnemonic devices are:

- "Every Good Bird Does Fly" (or "Every Good Boy Does Fine") for E-G-B-D-F, the five lines on the treble clef of the musical staff (the sentence makes sense; the sequence of letters doesn't)

- finding the "special" numbers in a series of numbers you want to remember—like your birthday in a friend's telephone number.

Do you use mnemonic devices? Do they make sense to you? This PSI will tell you how much your memory depends on things making sense.

You'll need some special materials for this PSI:

- scissors
- an 8½" x 11" sheet of stiff paper
- two brads
- a stopwatch or a timer

You'll be making two memory wheels. One will have three-letter words. The other will have three-letter nonsense syllables.

- Cut four circles out of the stiff paper. Each should be about 4" in diameter.
- Copy the words onto one circle, the syllables onto the other.

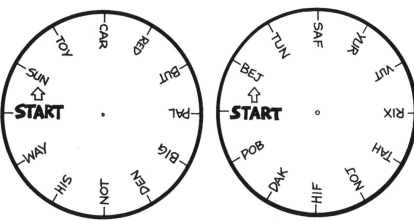

- Cut a small window in each of the other two circles, like this:

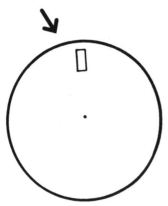

- Attach a window circle to the word circle with a brad. Put the brad in the very center so the wheel will turn. Attach the other window circle to the nonsense circle.

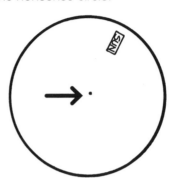

Now you're ready.

1. Put the window of the word wheel at START. Turn the wheel and study the words for one minute. When your time is up, write down as many words as you can remember:

_____ _____
_____ _____
_____ _____
_____ _____
_____ _____
_____ _____

2. Put the window of the nonsense wheel at START. Turn the wheel and study the nonsense syllables for one minute. When your time is up, write down as many nonsense syllables as you can remember:

_____ _____
_____ _____
_____ _____
_____ _____
_____ _____
_____ _____

WHAT'S YOUR STYLE?

Which did you remember better, the words or the nonsense syllables? Most people find it easier to remember the words.

Did you make up a system to remember the nonsense syllables? Most people find it easier to remember things that make sense to them.

> "One of the oddest things in life, I think, is the things one remembers."
>
> —*Agatha Christie, mystery writer*

If you remembered the nonsense syllables easily, you are not like most people! You have a more flexible memory system.

Find Out MORE

✳ Can you think of mnemonic devices in addition to the ones in this PSI? Maybe you could make up a card game using popular mnemonic devices. Write the first half of the mnemonic device on one card, and the second half on another card. Make as many sets of cards as you can. Your game could be a match-up game.

✳ Use what you've learned about memory systems to study for your next test. Arrange the information you need to know into a system that makes sense to you. (For example, some people use different ink or paper colors for different types of information.) When you take the test, it should be easier for you to recall what you need to know.

✳ Do you have trouble remembering certain things, like names or phone numbers? Develop a system for remembering these things. Ask other people for ideas.

> "I stored the fact...in the corner of my mind the way a squirrel stores a nut."
>
> —Sylvia Plath, poet

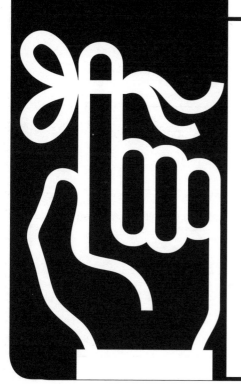

More Mnemonics

- the word "FACE" for the spaces on the treble clef of the musical staff (the notes for those spaces really spell the word—handy!)
- tying a "don't forget" string around your finger
- the rhyme, "30 days hath September," for remembering how many days are in the months of the year
- "Spring ahead, Fall back" for Daylight Savings Time changes
- "ROY G. BIV" for the colors of the spectrum (red, orange, yellow, green, blue, indigo, violet)
- "I before E, except after C" for spelling words
- "In fourteen hundred ninety-two, Columbus sailed the ocean blue" for that historic year

PSI #32

HOW OBSERVANT ARE YOU?

Do you notice things, especially small things that most people overlook? We all notice the unusual. If a flying saucer landed in your backyard, you couldn't miss it! But what about things that are routine or commonplace? It's easy to miss things we see every day—as this PSI will show.

Answer these questions about things that should be very familiar to you. Answer them from memory—no cheating!

1. What color are your best friend's eyes?

_____

2. Which direction does a record turn on a turntable, clockwise or counterclockwise?

_____

3. What color is the sofa in your best friend's house?

_____

4. What's the license plate number on your family car?

_____

5. How many trees are in your backyard?

_____

6. Does your teacher wear a wedding ring?

_____

7. What brand of pencil do you usually write with?

_____

8. Which direction do you face in your most recent school picture—right, left, or straight ahead?

_____

9. How many shelves are in your refrigerator?

_____

10. How many pictures hang on the wall of your own living room?

_____

11. What company publishes your math text book?

_____

12. What is the design on the bottom of your sneakers?

_____

13. What brand of milk does your family usually buy?

_____

14. Inside the jacket you usually wear, what does the label say?

_____

15. In your bathtub, is the hot-water knob to the right or left?

_____

> "The whole secret of the study of nature lies in learning how to use one's eyes."
>
> —George Sand (pseudonym of Amandine Aurore Lucie, Baronne Dudevant), writer

> "We are as much as we see."
>
> —Henry David Thoreau, writer

WHAT'S YOUR STYLE?

CHECK YOUR ANSWERS, THEN TOTAL THE NUMBER YOU GOT RIGHT.

- 10–15 right = NOTHING gets past you—you're Super-Observant
- 5–10 right = you're fairly observant
- fewer than 5 right = you need practice!

Find Out MORE

✷ Make up more questions like these and give them to your friends or family. Think of things they see every day but might not notice.

✷ Pick something about people or places that you often see but don't notice. (For example: the color of people's eyes, whether they wear a wedding ring or any other rings, the number of stories in a building, the number of windows in a room.) Try to notice that detail in the next 10 people or places you see.

PSI #33

DO YOU USE SELECTIVE ATTENTION?

When you talk on the phone to your best friend and your little sister bugs you, what do you do? You "tune out" your sister. What you're really doing is using *selective attention.* You're paying attention to the words coming through the phone and blocking out what your sister is saying or doing.

Selective attention means focusing on *relevant* (meaningful) information and ignoring *irrelevant* (meaningless) information. Using selective attention isn't always easy. Find out how skilled you are. For this PSI, you'll need seven or eight different colored pens, pencils, or crayons.

1. **Color each word any color besides the one it names. (For example, color GREEN red or purple.) Pick your colors randomly; don't think too much about them.**

PINK RED GREY
GREEN PURPLE
BLACK YELLOW
BLUE ORANGE
WHITE BLUE

2. **Look at the words and name the colors you see. DON'T name the words you read. This is harder than you think!**

WHAT'S YOUR STYLE?

Could you name the colors easily without getting confused by the words? In this example, the colors are relevant information; the words are irrelevant information.

This PSI shows how much reading has changed your life. You don't "see" things in the same way you once did. Show your colored-in words to a child who's old enough to know colors but doesn't yet know how to read. He or she will have no trouble naming the colors.

Find Out MORE

✳ Watch your favorite TV show. Pay attention to the background, the setting, the music, and what the characters are doing. Ignore what the characters are saying. Do you see things you normally would miss? Do you have a different understanding of what's going on in the show than you would if you were focusing on the words?

✳ Use selective attention when you do your homework. Block out distractions. Is this hard to do? Can you get rid of some distractions (TV, radio, breeze coming in the window) to make it easier?

✳ Choose a word (like "intrinsic," for example) or a thing (like a blue pickup truck) and make yourself very aware of it. Chances are you'll start hearing/ seeing your word/thing everywhere you go. (You may have noticed this in the past when you've learned a new

word or idea. Maybe you thought it was mysterious or magical, but it's really just selective attention at work.)

✳ Turn your selective attention into "collective" attention. Arrange to get together with a friend to share collections. Each of you should bring a collection that the other person doesn't have and isn't especially interested in. (For example, you collect baseball cards, and your friend collects stamps.) Look closely at your friend's collection while your friend looks at yours. Talk about what each of you "sees" in the other person's collection. Then tell what you "see" in your own collection. What does this tell you about selective attention? (Hint: All pennies look the same to a noncollector, but not to a collector.)

✳ Your room looks neat to you, but your parents think it's a mess. What does this have to do with selective attention?

SELECTIVE ATTENTION AND SURVIVAL

Selective attention can be a survival mechanism. For example, to us, ice is ice, and that's all we need to know. But to the Inuit, ice is an important part of life. Knowing about different kinds of ice, and being able to describe them accurately, is essential to survival. That's why we have one word for ice, and the Inuit have as many as 170! Here's a sampling:

- *salogok* is "young black ice"—thin, new, non-reflective ice. (This is the ice your parents complain about during winter driving.)

- *migalik* is "pancake ice"—round, flat pieces of young ice formed when ice cakes rotate and collide with one another.

- *eyechektakok* is a crack in the ice that keeps opening and closing.

There are times when noticing differences is vital to our survival, too. Here are some examples. Can you add to these lists?

> **"Are you a good witch, or a bad witch?"**
> —*Glinda to Dorothy in the film* The Wizard of Oz

ITEM	OKAY TYPE	NOT-OKAY TYPE
OAK	OAK TREE	POISON OAK
IVY	GRAPE IVY	POISON IVY
SPIDER	DADDY LONG LEGS	BLACK WIDOW
SNAKE	GARDEN SNAKE	RATTLESNAKE
MUSHROOMS	EDIBLE	POISONOUS
BERRIES	BLUEBERRIES	HOLLY BERRIES

PSI #34

WHAT'S YOUR LEARNING STYLE?

To learn, you depend on your senses to bring information to your brain. Most people tend to use one of their senses more than the others. Some people learn best by listening. They are called *auditory* learners. Other people learn best by reading or seeing pictures. They are *visual* learners. Still others learn best by touching and doing things. They are called *kinesthetic* learners.

Scientists and psychologists don't know why people use one sense more than the others. Maybe the sense they use the most just works better for them.

Knowing your learning style may help you to learn. It may also explain why some things just don't make sense to you.

For these questions, choose the first answer that comes to mind. Don't spend too much time thinking about any question.

1. Which way would you rather learn how a computer works?

   A. watching a movie about it

   B. listening to someone explain it

   C. taking the computer apart and trying to figure it out for yourself

2. Which would you prefer to read for fun?

   A. a travel book with a lot of pictures in it

   B. a mystery book with a lot of conversation in it

   C. a book where you answer questions and do puzzles

3. When you aren't sure how to spell a word, which of these are you most likely to do?

   A. write it out to see if it looks right

   B. sound it out

   C. write it out to sense if it feels right

4. If you were at a party, what would you be most likely to remember the next day?

   A. the faces of the people there, but not the names

   B. the names but not the faces

   C. the things you did and said while you were there

5. How would you rather study for a test?

   A. read notes, read headings in a book, look at diagrams and illustrations

   B. have someone ask you questions, or repeat facts silently to yourself

   C. write things out on index cards and make models or diagrams

6. When you see the word "d-o-g," what do you do first?

   A. think of a picture of a particular dog

   B. say the word "dog" to yourself silently

   C. sense the feeling of being with a dog (petting it, running with it, etc.)

7. What do you find most distracting when you are trying to concentrate?

    A. visual distractions

    B. noises

    C. other sensations like hunger, tight shoes, or worry

8. How do you prefer to solve a problem?

    A. make a list, organize the steps, and check them off as they are done

    B. make a few phone calls and talk to friends or experts

    C. make a model of the problem or walk through all the steps in your mind

9. Which are you most likely to do while standing in a long line at the movies?

    A. look at the posters advertising other movies

    B. talk to the person next to you

    C. tap your foot or move around in some other way

10. You have just entered a science museum. What will you do first?

    A. look around and find a map showing the locations of the various exhibits

    B. talk to a museum guide and ask about exhibits

    C. go into the first exhibit that looks interesting, and read directions later

11. When you are angry, which are you most likely to do?

    A. scowl

    B. shout or "blow up"

    C. stomp off and slam doors

12. When you are happy, what are you most likely to do?

    A. grin

    B. shout with joy

    C. jump for joy

13. Which would you rather go to?

    A. an art class

    B. a music class

    C. an exercise class

14. Which of these do you do when you listen to music?

    A. daydream (see images that go with the music)

    B. hum along

    C. move with the music, tap your foot, etc.

15. How would you rather tell a story?

    A. write it

    B. tell it out loud

    C. act it out

16. Which kind of restaurant would you rather not go to?

    A. one with the lights too bright

    B. one with the music too loud

    C. one with uncomfortable chairs

WHAT'S YOUR STYLE?

TOTAL YOUR A'S, B'S, AND C'S:

A'S	B'S	C'S

- If you scored mostly A's, you may have a visual learning style. You learn by seeing and looking.

- If you scored mostly B's, you may have an auditory learning style. You learn by hearing and listening.

- If you had mostly C's, you may have a kinesthetic learning style. You learn by touching and doing.

- If you circled more than one letter about the same number of times, you depend on more than one learning style.

It's not unusual to use different learning styles for different tasks. For instance, you might repeat your German lessons out loud to prepare for a test, but study your textbook to prepare for your math quiz. And you might repeat some experiments you did in class to prepare for your chemistry test.

In these cases, you're using an auditory style to learn a language. You're using a visual learning style to learn math. And you're using a kinesthetic style to learn chemistry. Each one helps you learn what you need to know.

"The more math you know, the more successful you'll be. It's a very powerful way to train your mind."
—Joyce O'Halloran, Ph.D., math professor

Find Out MORE

✶ The next time you study for a quiz or test, put into practice what you learned in this PSI. If your learning style is auditory, read out loud the information you need to know. If it's kinesthetic, make a model or do something practical that will help you learn the information. If it's visual, read a text and study illustrations.

✶ If you have to do a project in school, design one that fits your learning style.

"They know enough who know how to learn."
—Henry Brooks Adams, historian

ARE YOU A LONE LEARNER OR A TEAM PLAYER?

PSI #35

Some people like to solve problems by themselves.
Others work better in groups.
Which kind are you, a lone learner or a team player?

To do this PSI, you'll need two or three other people and a stopwatch or timer.

1. The Lone Learner Quiz

Choose one of the words from the list below. Set the watch or timer for five minutes. Start the timer, then write as many words as you can using the letters in the word you chose. The rules: These must be real words of two letters and up. Use only the letters in the word you chose. If there is only one "n" in that word, then you can use only one "n" in any word you write. But you can use the "n" in more than one word. Stop writing when your five minutes are up.

2. The Team Player Quiz

Form a group with two or more people. Choose one word from the list that none of you used in the Lone Learner Quiz. Now work together to come up with words using those letters. Put one person in charge of writing them down. Again, take five minutes.

PUBLISHING	**INSIGHTFUL**	**SCAVENGERS**	**PALINDROME**
GUIDELINES	**PERFECTION**	**TELEPHONES**	**DICTIONARY**

WHAT'S YOUR STYLE?

How many words did you come up with in the Lone Learner Quiz?

How many words did your team come up with in the Team Player Quiz?

Who made more words—you alone, or your team?

If your results seem unusual, you may want to try these tests a couple of times each, using different words.

Chances are your team came out ahead. But what about your personal performance? Did you come up with more words when you were working alone, or did working with a team "push" you to think of more words than you would have by yourself?

How did you feel when you were working alone? Maybe you felt confident and full of ideas. Maybe you felt unsure about how you were doing.

How did you feel when you were working with the group? Maybe it gave you lots of ideas. Maybe it distracted and frustrated you.

If you had more ideas and were happier working alone, then you're a loner when it comes to problem solving. But this doesn't mean that you're a loner all the time.

If you had more ideas and were happier working with the group, then you're a team player when it comes to problem solving. But this doesn't mean you won't want to work alone sometimes.

Find Out MORE

* The next time you have to do a group project in school, think of this PSI. If you're a team player, terrific! You'll enjoy working on the project, and you'll probably do your best work. If you're a lone learner, think of ways you can contribute to the project but still do some of the work by yourself. Try your best to work with the group as much as you can.

* What are some careers where people work alone? What careers require people to work with others? What's your problem-solving style? Can you see the connection?

* If you liked this PSI, you might enjoy playing Boggle, a word-finding game for two or more people. (Of course, you can practice playing it alone—but it's the most fun when it's played in teams.)

PSI #36

ARE YOU SUPERSTITIOUS?

Do you learn things on purpose, or by accident? Some examples of on-purpose learning include studying for a spelling test, doing drill-and-practice math problems, and drawing a map of Europe and labeling the capital cities. An example of "accidental" learning is deciding that your red shirt is "lucky" because you wear it one day and have a great day.

Of course, you know *intellectually* that the shirt didn't cause your great day. But *emotionally* it may seem that your red shirt is "lucky." And you may act on these feelings in the future, wearing your red shirt whenever you want to have a great day.

The belief in luck (good or bad) is called *superstition.* This PSI helps you find out how superstitious you are. Good luck!

Ask yourself these 12 questions. For each, check Yes or No.

1. Do you go out of your way to walk around ladders instead of under them?

Yes ☐   No ☐

2. Do you ever rearrange your room, change your hairstyle, or do other things in the hope of changing your luck?

Yes ☐   No ☐

3. Do you have a Good Luck Piece, like a rabbit's foot or a special coin or stone?

Yes ☐   No ☐

4. Do you feel a twinge of anxiety when a black cat crosses your path?

Yes ☐   No ☐

5. On Friday the 13th, are you a little more cautious than usual?

Yes ☐   No ☐

6. Do you feel that supporting an athletic team somehow helps them win?

Yes ☐   No ☐

7. Do you avoid stepping on cracks in the sidewalk?

Yes ☐   No ☐

8. If you broke a mirror, would your first thought be, "Oh, no, here come seven years of bad luck!"?

Yes ☐   No ☐

9. Do you have a lucky number?

Yes ☐   No ☐

10. Do you have a lucky color?

Yes ☐   No ☐

11. Do you regularly read your horoscope in the daily newspaper or in magazines?

Yes ☐   No ☐

12. Do you sometimes feel that it's luckier to do things in a certain order—for example, putting your left shoe on first, or brushing your teeth before you comb your hair?

Yes ☐   No ☐

WHAT'S YOUR STYLE?

TOTAL YOUR YES AND NO RESPONSES.

YES'S	NO'S

- 10–12 No's mean you're not at all superstitious
- 8–9 No's mean you're not very superstitious
- 5–7 No's mean you're about average when it comes to being superstitious
- 3–4 No's mean you're somewhat superstitious
- 0–2 No's mean you're very superstitious

"A few people will be at the right place at the right time by luck, but most people win by building the right place themselves and spending a heck of a lot of time there."

—Marilyn vos Savant, American columnist (listed under "Highest IQ" in the Guinness Book of World Records)

Find Out MORE

* Find out about superstitions in other cultures and countries. Do they seem even stranger than the ones you're used to? For example: In Japan, there is a superstition about the number 4—one should avoid saying it because it means death! Greeks avoid saying "five," but people of the Muslim faith believe that an outstretched hand with five fingers spread keeps evil away. In Italy, to offer someone salt is bad luck. And so on.... If you're fascinated by superstitions, you'll probably find this book good reading: *A Dictionary of Superstitions* by Iona Opie (Oxford University Press, 2005).

* The next time you watch a baseball game, notice the many little habits of the batters. Many of these reflect superstitions they developed after hitting home runs—another example of accidental learning.

* If you have a personal superstition that's unique to you (as far as you know), try to remember how it got started. Ask your family members and friends about their superstitions. You may want to collect unusual ones in a notebook.

* Have a costume party where everyone comes dressed as a superstition. Make up games to go along with this theme. For example, tape yarn to the floor for "cracks," turn off the lights, and have people "freeze" when the lights come back on—if you're stepping on a "crack," you're out! (A "lucky" day to schedule this party might be Friday the 13th.)

SUPERSTITION SOURCES

Invent your own logical or funny explanations about how some traditional superstitions may have gotten started. For example: "Once upon a time, someone saw many people walking under ladders and getting paint spilled on their heads. From this came the superstition, 'It's bad luck to walk under ladders.'"

Here are more superstitions to explain:

- It's bad luck to open an umbrella in the house.
- It's good luck if a white cat crosses your path, bad luck if a black cat does.
- It's good luck to carry a rabbit's foot (unless you're the rabbit!).
- It's good luck to hang a horseshoe over a door (just make sure it's securely attached, or it could be bad luck!).
- It's good luck to find a four-leaf clover.
- Seven is a lucky number.
- Thirteen is an unlucky number.
- Friday the 13th is an unlucky day.
- Breaking a mirror brings seven years of bad luck.
- If you spill salt, you must throw a pinch over your left shoulder or you'll have bad luck.

What other superstitions can you think of and explain?

WHAT TO DO WHEN SUPERSTITIONS AREN'T FUN ANYMORE

Sometimes accidental learning can cause problems. For example, a girl is asleep in her room when lightning strikes a tree nearby. The noise frightens her awake, and now she's afraid to go into her room at night.

Sometimes people get stuck in rituals—certain ways of doing things. They start believing that rituals can make something good happen, or keep something bad from happening. For example, a boy thinks he has to walk backward into math class before taking a test. He feels weird about doing it, his friends make fun of him for doing it, and his teacher has asked him to stop doing it, but he does it anyway! The boy believes that walking backward into class helps him with his math tests. He thinks that if he stops doing it, he might fail.

If you find yourself getting bogged down by fears or rituals, tell an adult you trust and can talk to. Don't let superstitions take charge of your life!

SPECIAL STYLES

NOTE: This part of *Psychology for Kids Vol. 1* focuses on unique and unusual abilities. Some people believe that these abilities are real. Others aren't sure. Still others are convinced that they're a lot of nonsense.

All we really know about these abilities is that they're interesting. An intelligent person investigates everything with an open mind. Often, things which seem mystical or magical at first are eventually explained in a logical fashion. For example, when people first started learning to read and write, these activities seemed mystical and magical to people who couldn't do them. One day, we may arrive at a perfectly logical explanation for extra-sensory perception—if we let ourselves explore the possibilities.

Even if these unique and unusual abilities are real, they aren't common. You may not have any of them. If it appears as if you do have one (or some), you may want to find out more about it. Talk to your parents or teachers, or ask a librarian for help in finding books and articles. Meanwhile, have fun with these PSIs. And keep an open mind!

DO YOU HAVE A PHOTOGRAPHIC MEMORY?

People with photographic memories can look at an image and "see" it again later, down to every last detail. For example, a person with a photographic memory could tell you the last word on page 358 of a 700-page book she or he had just read, without looking back to find it. Individuals with this ability have been known to memorize whole telephone directories, re-create paintings from memory, and perform other amazing feats.

For many years, psychologists questioned whether there was such a thing as photographic memory. Now most psychologists agree that it does exist. But it's still very hard to measure and test. And it's not easy to tell the difference between a photographic memory, a very good memory, and the ability to see afterimages.

PART I: Look at this figure under bright lights for about 30 seconds. (Find a spot near the center and focus on it.) Then immediately stare at the white space below the figure. Do you see a word form there? This is called an *afterimage*.

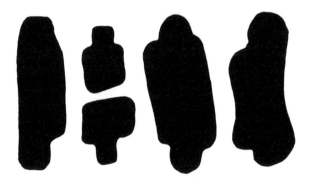

PART II: Take 45 seconds to memorize this quotation by Albert Einstein.

"Do not pride yourself on the few great men who, over the centuries, have been born on on your earth through no merit of yours. Reflect, rather, on on how you treated them at the time, and how you have followed their teachings."

Now write it on a separate sheet of paper, exactly as you memorized it.

PART III: Think of something you memorized a long time ago and know very well. This might be a short prayer, a creed, a pledge (like the United States Pledge of Allegiance), an oath (like the Boy Scout Oath), or something similar. Write it backward. Include punctuation.

WHAT'S YOUR STYLE?

- **Part I tested your ability to see afterimages. When you looked away from the figure to the white space, you should have seen the word HI in big black letters.**

- **Part II tested your memory power. If you have a superior memory, you may have remembered and written the whole quotation. But did you remember and write the mistakes? (What mistakes? Look at the quotation again.)**

- **Part III tested your photographic memory. If you truly have a photographic memory, you were able to write what you had memorized backward with no trouble. If you don't have a photographic memory, it probably took you a very long time.**

Most people do fine on the afterimages test, so-so on the superior memory test, and not so well on the photographic memory test. That's because photographic memory is rare, though it seems to be more common in young children than adults.

Find Out MORE

✻ If you think you have a photographic memory, talk to your parents, teacher, or school counselor. There are tests you can take to find out more about this special ability.

✻ Maybe you don't have a photographic memory, but you're interested in this unusual skill. Check your library for books on photographic memory. Perhaps you can "develop" one.

PSI #38

DO YOU HAVE ESP?

ESP stands for *extra-sensory perception.* It means knowing or learning about something without using your five senses (sight, hearing, touch, taste, smell). For example, someone with ESP might know that the phone is going to ring before it does. He or she might know what another person is thinking. ESP is often thought of as a "hunch" or "intuition."

J. B. Rhine, former Director of the Parapsychology Laboratory at Duke University, did experiments on ESP in the 1930s. He used special cards called Zener cards. Rhine's studies seemed to prove that ESP really exists. But other people have repeated Rhine's experiments and found no evidence of ESP.

Is ESP a special gift, or does it just tap into brain abilities that everybody has but few people use? Nobody knows. Do you have ESP? Here's a way to find out.

PART I: Make your own deck of Zener cards. You'll need 25 white index cards and something to write with. A black marker works best.

You'll also need someone to help you with this experiment. One of you will be the sender, and the other will be the receiver.

Draw each of the symbols below on five cards.

The sender and the receiver sit across from each other at a desk or a table. The sender shuffles the Zener cards, places the deck face down, and draws the top card. The sender concentrates on the card, and the receiver tries to sketch the symbol the sender is looking at. Then the sender goes on to the next card, and so on through the deck of 25.

Take turns being the sender and the receiver.

PART II: You'll need a magazine for this experiment. Choose one with lots of pictures.

You'll also need a partner to help you. One of you will be the sender, and the other will be the receiver.

Sit across from each other at a desk or a table. Put a screen or another barrier between you. (A board from a board game makes a good barrier.)

The sender opens the magazine and concentrates on a picture, thinking about the colors and shapes he or she sees. The receiver relaxes and draws whatever comes to mind, without trying to figure out what the sender is sending.

Try this with several pictures. Take turns being the sender and the receiver.

> *"There is nothing impossible in the existence of the supernatural: its existence seems to me decidedly probable."*
>
> —George Santayana,
> poet and philosopher

WHAT'S YOUR STYLE?

- **PART I:** If the receiver drew some of the same images the sender was sending, ESP may be at work.

- **PART II:** If the receiver's drawing was close to the actual picture the sender was sending, then one or both of you may be using ESP.

If you do these experiments several times, you should get some idea of your ESP powers. Remember, though, that ESP is very rare—if it exists at all.

Find Out MORE

✳ After doing these experiments, you may think you have ESP. Read more about this unusual ability. Ask your librarian to point you toward books and articles on the subject. You'll probably find quite a few—some saying that ESP exists, and some saying it doesn't.

✳ If you like reading about ESP, and you enjoy fantasy and science fiction, check out some of the Darkover novels by Marion Zimmer Bradley.

✳ The Rhine Research Center is a not-for-profit organization that does ongoing research on ESP and related subjects. The center offers a list of recommended books and links on parapsychology and other interesting materials. For more information about the center, or to request a copy of their booklist, write or call: Rhine Research Center, 2741 Campus Walk Avenue, Building 500, Durham, NC 27705; telephone (919) 309-4600. Or visit them online (www.rhine.org).

✳ For a list of U.S. and international sources on parapsychology, write or call: Parapsychology Foundation, PO Box 1562, New York, NY 10021; telephone (212) 628-1550. Or visit them online (www.parapsychology.org).

PSI #39

ARE YOU CLAIRVOYANT?

Researchers have identified three types of ESP: *telepathy, clairvoyance,* and *precognition.* Telepathy is mind-to-mind communication. PSI #38 tests your telepathic abilities. Clairvoyance is the ability to "see" things, people, and events that are not in your range of vision. This PSI tests your clairvoyance. Precognition is the ability to see the future. Find out about precognition in PSI #40.

You'll need a timer, writing paper, and something to write with. You'll also need a partner. One of you will be the sender, and the other will be the receiver.

The receiver stays in a room while the sender goes to some other location. The receiver shouldn't know where the sender goes.

The sender concentrates on sending a "mental message" to the receiver. The message should be about the place the sender is in. The sender also does some simple activity—like writing a description of her or his location, or drawing a picture of it.

After three minutes, the sender returns to the room. The receiver then describes a location and activity. The sender compares this description to the place he or she was in. Are there any similarities?

Try this experiment several times, with the sender going to several different places. Take turns being the sender and the receiver.

"While parapsychology and [related] research are in themselves fascinating, their real value lies in part in their ability to point out inadequacies in our current belief systems."

—*Dr. Barbara Clark, educator, author of* Growing Up Gifted

WHAT'S YOUR STYLE?

Did you and your partner know each other's locations and activities? If so, you may be clairvoyant. But a few attempts won't prove or disprove clairvoyance. In fact, a few attempts won't prove anything!

Other factors may be at work. For example:

- **Maybe you're telepathic—maybe you can read your partner's mind!**

- **If you know your partner well, then perhaps it was easy to guess where your partner went and what he or she did there.**

- **Maybe, given the time and place you did this experiment, only a few options were available to your partner, and it wasn't hard to figure out which ones she or he chose.**

- **Maybe you peeked and saw where your partner went and what you partner did. (Do the experiment again, only this time, NO PEEKING!)**

- **Maybe what seems like clairvoyance was pure chance.**

Find Out MORE

✱ If you think you might be clairvoyant, find out more about this ability. Check your library for books and articles on clairvoyance.

✱ The Committee for the Skeptical Inquiry (CSI) was formed in 1977 by a group of prominent journalists and scientists who don't believe in things like clairvoyance. Its members believe that claims of paranormal abilities and events are against science and harmful to society. CSI publishes a quarterly magazine called *The Skeptical Inquirer*.

For more information, write or call: The Skeptical Inquirer, PO Box 703, Amherst, NY 14226; telephone 1-800-634-1610. Or visit them online (www.csicop.org).

"There are no unnatural or supernatural phenomena, only very large gaps in our knowledge of what is natural....We should strive to fill those gaps of ignorance."
—*Edgar Mitchell*, Apollo 14 *astronaut*

CAN YOU PREDICT THE FUTURE?

PSI #40

MIT meteorologist Edward Lorenz wanted to know why the weather is so unpredictable. In 1963, he came up with a theory to explain this puzzle. His theory is called the "Butterfly Effect." The theory states that it doesn't matter how many weather stations there are, or where they are; you still can't predict the weather more than a month or so ahead. Even if you know all about atmospheric conditions at a given point in time, you can't predict what conditions will be like in the future. Why? Because, the theory says, even the smallest change in conditions at the beginning of events might be enough to change the whole result. Lorenz used the example of something as small as one butterfly flapping its wings. That's how his theory got its name.

If we can't predict the weather, how can we possibly predict the future? Some people believe that we can't. Others believe that we can. Astrologers and psychics regularly predict events like airplane crashes and earthquakes. But we must remember that WRONG predictions get very little attention, while RIGHT predictions are put in the spotlight, if not on the front page of the daily newspaper.

If you believe that the future is predictable, then you must also assume certain things about reality. For example, you must assume that events are already "fixed in time" and aren't affected by anything—including a butterfly's flapping wings.

Think of four people you see every day. Predict what color each will wear each day on the next four days. (This might be easy because you already know what these people usually wear.) *The rules:* Don't count blue jeans for blue. And don't tell the people you're observing that you're doing this experiment. That might affect what they choose

to wear. Record your predictions and observations on the Color Prediction Chart on page 117. The following sample shows you how.

COLOR PREDICTION CHART

Name of Person	Day 1 Predicted Color	Day 1 Actual Color	Day 2 Predicted Color	Day 2 Actual Color	Day 3 Predicted Color
Jan	red	red	green	blue	
Jon	white	red	red	white	
Tammy	green	blue	orange	orange	
Sam	yellow	yellow	green	white	
Chris	red	blue	green	green	
Sue	blue	white	blue	yellow	

WHAT'S YOUR STYLE?

Like the sample chart, your Color Prediction Chart probably shows at least a few "hits" (correct predictions) and several "misses" (incorrect predictions). Results like these are about average. Anyone just guessing could do about the same. In other words, there's no proof here of "predictability." To claim you can predict the future, you'd have to get every person's color right on every day.

What if your Color Prediction Chart shows more hits than misses? Hmmm....

Can you predict the future? Do you believe that others can?

From *Psychology for Kids Vol. 1* by Jonni Kincher, copyright © 2008. Free Spirit Publishing Inc., Minneapolis, MN; 800-735-7323; www.freespirit.com.

COLOR PREDICTION CHART

Name of Person	Day 1 Predicted Color	Day 1 Actual Color	Day 2 Predicted Color	Day 2 Actual Color	Day 3 Predicted Color	Day 3 Actual Color	Day 4 Predicted Color	Day 4 Actual Color

Find Out MORE

✱ Try other experiments in predicting the future. Predict who will win your school football or basketball game. Predict who will win the next local election. How accurate are your predictions?

✱ Many people enjoy saving predictions published at the beginning of the year, then reviewing them at yearend. This could be a fun tradition to start in your family. Or make and review predictions of your own.

✱ Think about an event in your life that was changed by a "butterfly." What does this tell you about decisions that may seem unimportant?

✱ Read the short story by Ray Bradbury called "A Sound of Thunder." You can find it in his collection called *Bradbury Classic Stories 1: From the Golden Apples of the Sun and R Is for Rocket* (Bantam, 1990) and also in *The Stories of Ray Bradbury* (Alfred A. Knopf, 1980).

✱ The Parapsychological Association is an affiliate of the American Association for the Advancement of Science, which also includes "mainstream" sciences like biology. The Parapsychological Association is considered to be a relatively "neutral" organization—it isn't strongly for or against the possibility of unusual abilities like clairvoyance and predicting the future. To find out more, write: Parapsychological Association, Inc., 1390 N. McDowell Boulevard, Suite G-208, Petaluma, CA 94954. Or visit them online (www.parapsych.org).

THE BUTTERFLY EFFECT AND BACK TO THE FUTURE

The sample chart on page 116 shows a person named Jon putting on a red shirt instead of a white shirt (the predicted color). Let's pretend that we know the whole story behind this decision.

Maybe Jon did put on a white shirt when he got up. For a while, the prediction was "correct." But then Jon spilled syrup on his white shirt at breakfast, and that caused him to change into the red one.

Why did he spill the syrup? Because he was in a hurry...because he got up late...because he forgot to set his alarm...because he was too tired when he went to bed last night...because he stayed up past his bedtime drawing another map for his geography class...because his dog ate the first map he drew...because his sister left a salami sandwich sitting on it.

That salami sandwich was like a butterfly flapping its wings. It changed conditions enough to turn a hit prediction into a miss.

Maybe you've seen the Back to the Future movies starring Michael J. Fox. These movies are really about the Butterfly Effect. What's the "butterfly" in each movie?

GRAND SCORE SHEET

Get the "big picture" of your personal style. Enter the results from all your PSIs onto this Grand Score Sheet. Keep a copy in a safe place. After a year or two, take the PSIs again. How have you changed? How have you stayed the same?

YOUR NAME _____   **TODAY'S DATE** _____

YOUR ATTITUDES

PSI #1: ARE YOU AN OPTIMIST OR A PESSIMIST?

Optimist ☐   Pessimist ☐

PSI #2: ARE YOU AN INTROVERT OR AN EXTROVERT?

Introvert ☐   Extrovert ☐

PSI #3: CHOOSE YOUR SUPERPOWERS

My choices: _____

_____

_____

What my choices say about me: _____

_____

_____

Careers to consider: _____

_____

_____

PSI #4: DO YOU THINK IN STEREOTYPES?

Yes ☐   No ☐   Sometimes ☐

PSI #5: WHAT ARE YOUR LIMITS?

I place few ☐   some ☐   many ☐
limits on myself

PSI #6: BOOST YOUR MIND POWER

My Mind Power is strong ☐   VERY strong ☐

PSI #7: WHAT DO YOU SEE?

Here are some things the inkblots say about me:

_____

_____

_____

_____

_____

_____

YOUR FEELINGS

PSI #8: HOW MANY PERSONAS DO YOU HAVE?

My persona (or personas): _____

_____

_____

How many? _____

Positive or negative? _____

PSI #9: THUMB THEORIES

What my thumb says about me: _____

_____

_____

PSI #10: WHAT SORT OF MORPH ARE YOU?

Endomorph ☐   Mesomorph ☐   Ectomorph ☐

PSI #11: WHAT DO DOODLES DO?

My need to achieve (nAch) is:

☐ very high

☐ high

☐ somewhat high

☐ neutral

☐ somewhat low

☐ low

☐ very low

PSI #12: WHAT DOES YOUR SIGNATURE SAY ABOUT YOU?

What my signature says about me: _____

_____

_____

PSI #13: YOUR COLORFUL PERSONALITY

What my favorite color says about me: _____

_____

_____

PSI #14: MOOD MUSIC

This is the kind of music I like: _____

_____

_____

This is what it says about me: _____

_____

_____

PSI #15: MOOD FOOD

Here are some of my food feelings: _____

_____

_____

YOUR SOCIAL STYLES

PSI #16: WHAT MAKES YOU ACT THE WAY YOU DO?

Intrinsic motivation ☐   Extrinsic motivation ☐

PSI #17: SETTING PRIORITIES

I am good ☐   okay ☐   not so good ☐

at setting priorities.

PSI #18: ARE YOU HABIT-BOUND?

My habit-bound rating (1 = very habit-bound)

10   **5**   **1**

●————————————————○————————————————●

PSI #19: ARE YOU SUGGESTIBLE?

Somewhat ☐   Very ☐   Not at all ☐

PSI #20: ARE YOU A LEADER?

I need more confidence in myself ☐

I need more confidence in others ☐

I have a realistic view of myself and others ☐

PSI #21: WHAT BODY LANGUAGE DO YOU SPEAK?

What my body language says about me:

Handshake: _____

_____

Sitting: _____

_____

Standing: _____

_____

Sitting at desk/table: _____

_____

Gestures: _____

_____

Other people

always ☐   almost always ☐   sometimes ☐

hardly ever ☐   almost never ☐

understand the message I mean to send.

PSI #22: YOUR COMMUNICATION STYLE 1

Ego state: parent ☐   adult ☐   child ☐

Sensory mode favored:

hearing ☐   seeing ☐   feeling ☐

PSI #23: YOUR COMMUNICATION STYLE 2

Positive self-talk ☐   Negative self-talk ☐

Very persuasive ☐   Not very persuasive ☐

YOUR CREATIVE STYLES

PSI #24: ARE YOU RIGHT-BRAINED OR LEFT-BRAINED?

Right-brained ☐   Left-brained ☐   Equal ☐

PSI #25: HOW INVENTIVE ARE YOU?

I'm more inventive than I thought I was ☐

I always knew I was inventive ☐

PSI #26: WHAT'S YOUR C.Q.?

My Creativity Quotient: _____

What it means: _____

_____

_____

PSI #27: TEST YOUR CREATIVITY

Fluency score: _____

Flexibility score: _____

Originality score: _____

Elaboration score: _____

Total creativity score: _____

My creativity rating (10 = very creative)

10 ———————— 5 ———————— 1

YOUR THINKING STYLES

PSI #28: ARE YOU A REAL GENIUS?

My Genius Score: _____

What it means: _____

_____

_____

PSI #29: WHO'S SMART?

My special intelligences: _____

_____

_____

PSI #30: ARE YOU A CRITICAL THINKER?

My critical thinking score: _____

What it means: _____

_____

_____

PSI #31: HOW'S YOUR MEMORY?

My memory system: _____

_____

_____

YOUR LEARNING STYLES

PSI #32: HOW OBSERVANT ARE YOU?

My score: _____

What it means: _____

_____

PSI #33: DO YOU USE SELECTIVE ATTENTION?

Yes ☐   No ☐   Sometimes ☐

PSI #34: WHAT'S YOUR LEARNING STYLE?

Visual ☐   Auditory ☐   Kinesthetic ☐

Check one, two, or all three.

PSI #35: ARE YOU A LONE LEARNER OR A TEAM PLAYER?

Lone Learner ☐   Team Player ☐

PSI #36: ARE YOU SUPERSTITIOUS?

Yes ☐   No ☐   About average ☐

SPECIAL STYLES

PSI #37: DO YOU HAVE A PHOTOGRAPHIC MEMORY?

Afterimages: Yes ☐   No ☐

Superior memory: Yes ☐   No ☐

Photographic memory: Yes ☐   No ☐

PSI #38: DO YOU HAVE ESP?

Yes ☐   No ☐   Maybe ☐

PSI #39: ARE YOU CLAIRVOYANT?

Yes ☐   No ☐   Maybe ☐

PSI #40: CAN YOU PREDICT THE FUTURE?

Yes ☐   No ☐   Maybe ☐

WHAT'S YOUR STYLE?

If you take a look at your Grand Score Sheet, you should find a reasonably accurate description of your personal style—IF you've answered the PSI questions as honestly as you can. You'll probably see some strengths and some weaknesses, some places where you shine and others that need a little polishing. In other words, you'll see a picture of balance.

Think about what you've learned about yourself. What's your best trait? What's your worst trait? What's the connection between the two? Often, our best and worst traits are closely related—they're just opposite sides of the same coin.

For example, someone who is very organized may be a bit selfish about letting other people borrow things. Or someone who has a disorganized and sloppy style might be very generous. The pessimist who is always finding the bad side of things may be the one to spot potential problems in time to prevent them.

Consider some of the things you think are negative about you. How might you turn them into positives? For example, don't think of yourself as a pessimist. Instead, think of yourself as a good "problem-finder." And take steps to become a good problem-solver, too.

YIN-YANG AND YOU

The ancient Chinese symbol of *yin-yang* tells a story of balance, opposites, and change.

The dark "fish" (yin) is the creative force. It stands for all that is mysterious, dark, cold, night, wintry, withdrawn. The light "fish" (yang) is the active force. It stands for light, sun, day, heat, summer, drought, fire. When each "fish" reaches its very largest size, it turns into the opposite color.

This symbol shows that nothing is all good or all bad, all dark or all light, all happy or all sad. All things exist only in relation to their opposites. If we had only the daytime, we wouldn't appreciate the light, because we wouldn't know the darkness.

The small dark spot in the light, and the small light spot in the dark, stand for the seeds of change. Everything can become its opposite. Within failure rests the seed of success—if you know how to learn from the failure. Within success rests the seed of failure—if you don't grow and change with the times.

The yin-yang symbol reminds us that we need balance in all parts of our lives.

WHAT TO DO WITH WHAT YOU'VE LEARNED

The good things you've learned about yourself can help you get through some of your hard times. They can give you something to hold on to—an emotional "anchor." For example, you can remind yourself that you're persistent and think of all the ways that persistence pays. Or you can pride yourself on being creative and a critical thinker.

The not-so-good things you've learned about yourself can guide you out of problems. Is one of your negative traits making the problem worse, or holding you back in some way? If you take responsibility for all of your characteristics, you can do something to change them.

Try to treat problems as chances to change. Remember the yin-yang symbol: Negatives often become positives. Dark turns into light.

INVENTING YOUR OWN REALITY

The most important question to ask yourself isn't "What's my personal style?" Instead, it's "Does my style match my intentions?" In other words, are you the person you want to be? Are you the way you are *on purpose*? Your personal style is your own. You create it, and you live with its results. You actually invent your own reality.

Are you the person you want to be? If not, what are you going to do about it? You can start by making a list of people you admire and the reasons you admire them. Your list will give you some hints about how you want to be. Your goal? To become the kind of person you admire.

You're already partway there. Keep up the good work!

> "You never know for whom you toil, who will reap the benefit of your work, who will grow in the nurturing of your giving, or who will respond to your being or having been. All you can do is commit to a dream, work hard, and act like someone who is the way you want to be."
>
> —Dr. David Viscott, psychiatrist and nationally known radio host

READ MORE ABOUT IT

If the PSIs in *Psychology for Kids Vol. 1* left you hungry for more, read on! Here's a list of books I know and like. Almost all of them are "do stuff" books; a few are fun, fact-filled reading.

Aha! Gotcha and Aha! Insight by Martin Gardner (Washington, DC: Mathematical Association of America, 2006). Fascinating paradoxes, puzzles, and weird (but true) logic. A feast for anyone who loves brain teasers.

Big Secrets by William Poundstone (New York: Quill Paperbacks, 1985), *Bigger Secrets* by William Poundstone (Boston: Houghton-Mifflin Co., 1989), and *Biggest Secrets* by William Poundstone (New York: William Morrow & Co., 1993). What's the secret formula for Coca-Cola? How are playing cards marked? These books are packed with answers to intriguing questions—perfect for the "James Bond" part of your personality. Each is an intriguing read from beginning to end.

Drawing on the Artist Within by Betty Edwards (New York: Simon & Schuster, Inc., 1987) and *The New Drawing on the Right Side of the Brain: A Course in Enhancing Creativity and Artistic Confidence* by Betty Edwards, Revised and Expanded Edition (New York: Jeremy P. Tarcher/Putnam, 1999). Don't be fooled by the titles; these books aren't just for people who are interested in art. Each includes intriguing exercises that show you how your brain and perceptions work. You'll learn to "see" everything around you in a whole new way!

Drawing with Children by Mona Brookes (Los Angeles: Jeremy P. Tarcher, 1996). This book is really for everyone who has ever wanted to draw. The method outlined by Mona Brookes has also been shown to improve concentration and visualization, problem-solving skills, and shape discrimination that aids reading.

The Great Brain Book: An Inside Look at the Inside of Your Head by HP Newquist (New York: Scholastic, 2005). Ever wonder how your brain works? This engaging book provides a complete picture of the brain's anatomy, and you'll even learn the real cause of brain freeze!

A Kick in the Seat of the Pants by Roger von Oech (New York: HarperCollins, 1986) and *A Whack on the Side of the Head: How You Can Be More Creative* by Roger von Oech, Revised Edition (New York: Business Plus, 2008). Two books full of whimsical ideas, crazy questions, puzzles, and interesting trivia about what makes you creative—and what keeps you from being creative.

You're Smarter Than You Think by Thomas Armstrong (Minneapolis: Free Spirit Publishing, 2002). Are you "word smart," "picture smart," or "people smart"? This book, with lots of quizzes, lists, and examples, can help you discover all the ways you are intelligent.

BIBLIOGRAPHY

Adams, James L., *Conceptual Block-busting: A Guide to Better Ideas,* 3rd ed. (Reading, MA: Addison-Wesley, 1990).

Anastasi, Anne, *Psychological Testing,* 6th ed. (New York: Macmillan, 1989).

Bandler, Richard, and John Grinder, *Frogs into Princes* (Moab, UT: Real People Press, 1979).

Berne, Eric, *Games People Play* (New York: Ballantine, 1985).
——*What Do You Say After You Say Hello?* (New York: Bantam, 1984).

Birren, Faber, *Color* (Secaucus, NJ.: Citadel Press, 1984).

Cerf, Christopher, and Victor Navasky, *The Experts Speak* (New York: Pantheon Books, 1984).

Edwards, Betty, *Drawing on the Artist Within* (New York: Simon & Schuster, 1987).
——*Drawing on the Right Side of the Brain* (Los Angeles: Jeremy P. Tarcher, Inc., 1989).

Gardner, Howard, *Frames of Mind* (New York: Basic Books, 1993).

Gardner, Martin, *Aha! Gotcha: Paradoxes to Puzzle and Delight* (New York: W.H. Freeman & Co., 1982).

Grinder, John, and Richard Bandler, *The Structure of Magic II* (Palo Alto, CA: Science & Behavior Books, 1976).
——*Trance-formations* (Moab, UT: Real People Press, 1981).

Kriegel, Robert, Ph.D. and Marilyn Harris Kriegel, Ph.D., *The C Zone: Peak Performance Under Pressure* (New York: Fawcett, 1985).

Poundstone, William, *Big Secrets* (New York: Quill Paperbacks, 1985).
——*Bigger Secrets* (Boston: Houghton-Mifflin Co., 1989).

Russell, Peter, *The Brain Book* (New York: E.P. Dutton, 1984).

Samuels, Mike, and Nancy Samuels, *Seeing with the Mind's Eye* (New York: Random House, 1975).

Wallace, Irving, and David Wallechinsky, Amy Wallace, and Sylvia Wallace, *The Book of Lists 2* (New York: William Morrow and Company, Inc., 1980).

INDEX

ABOUT THE AUTHOR

Jonni Kincher was born in Oklahoma and grew up in Colorado and California. She received her education in psychology at California State University, San Bernardino.

Her interest in psychology began when she was in third grade, but there weren't many psychology books for young children "back then," so she designed special courses in academic psychology for third grade through high school and created her own materials.

She began teaching "Psychology for Kids Playshops" so "kids" could use their natural curiosity about themselves to learn the basics of psychology as an academic discipline and thus be introduced to another area of study in the social sciences. The ideas and materials for her books were developed and tested in the Playshops.

Jonni continues to teach, learn, write, and create art. Her family has grown from a husband, John, and three sons—Adam, Joe, and Travis—to include the daughters she always wanted in the form of her daughters-in-law, Amy and Jolie.

She also is the author of the award-winning *Psychology for Kids Vol. 2: 40 Fun Experiments That Help You Learn About Others.*

More Great Books from Free Spirit

Psychology for Kids Vol. 2
40 Fun Experiments That Help You Learn About Others (Updated Edition)
by Jonni Kincher

Are people more logical or emotional? Do males and females see things differently? Can we shape other people's behavior? Based on science and sound psychological concepts and research, 40 interesting experiments make it fun for kids to learn about what makes people tick. Each experiment sharpens young people's skills as experimenters, researchers, and observers of human nature. The more teens find out about others, the more they learn about themselves. The included CD-ROM (for Windows and Macintosh) features all of the reproducible experiments from the book. For ages 12 & up.
128 pp.; softcover; illust.; 8½" x 11"

The Kid's Guide to Service Projects
Over 500 Service Ideas for Young People Who Want to Make a Difference (Updated 2nd Edition)
by Barbara A. Lewis

Hundreds of ideas for service projects, from simple to large-scale community efforts. Topics include animals, crime fighting, the environment, friendship, hunger, literacy, politics and government, and transportation. Endorsed by Youth Service America. For ages 10 & up.
160 pp.; softcover; 2-color; illust.; 6" x 9"

You're Smarter Than You Think
A Kid's Guide to Multiple Intelligences
by Thomas Armstrong, Ph.D.

Howard Gardner's theory of multiple intelligences has revolutionized the way we think about being smart. Written by an award-winning author and leading expert on multiple intelligences, this book helps kids identify their own learning strengths, build other intelligences, and use all eight at school, at home, and in life. For ages 8–12.
192 pp.; softcover; illust.; 7" x 9"

Fighting Invisible Tigers
Stress Management for Teens (Revised & Updated Third Edition)
by Earl Hipp

Stress is something we all experience. But research suggests that adolescents are affected by it in unique ways that can increase impulsivity and risky behaviors. This book offers proven techniques that teens can use to deal with stressful situations in school, at home, and among friends. They'll find current information on how stress affects health and decision making and learn stress-management skills to handle stress in positive ways—including assertiveness, positive self-talk, time management, relaxation exercises, and much more. For ages 11 & up.
144 pp.; softcover; illust.; 6" x 9"

What Do You Really Want?
How to Set a Goal and Go for It!
by Beverly K. Bachel, with a special note from Ann Bancroft, polar explorer

Setting and sticking to goals can ease stress and anxiety, boost concentration, and make life more satisfying. Written especially for teens, this step-by-step guide to goal setting helps teens articulate their goals and put them in writing, set priorities and deadlines, overcome obstacles, cope with roadblocks, build a support system, use positive self-talk, celebrate their successes, and more. For ages 11 & up.
144 pp.; softcover; illust.; 6" x 9"

Real Kids, Real Stories, Real Change
Courageous Actions Around the World
by Garth Sundem
Foreword by Bethany Hamilton

Ten-year-old Jean-Dominic won a battle against pesticides—and the cancer they caused in his body. Six-year-old Ryan raised $800,000 to drill water wells in Africa. Eleven-year-old Tilly saved lives in Thailand by warning people that a tsunami was coming. Fifteen-year-old Malika fought against segregation in her Alabama town. And twelve-year-old Haruka invented a new environmentally friendly way to scoop dog poop. With the right role models, any child can be a hero. Thirty true stories profile kids who used their heads, their hearts, their courage, and sometimes their stubbornness to help others and do extraordinary things. As young readers meet these boys and girls from around the world, they may wonder, "What kind of hero lives inside of me?" For ages 9–13.
176 pp.; softcover; 2-color; 5¼" x 7½"

100 Things Guys Need to Know
by Bill Zimmerman

Advice for guys on all kinds of issues, from family life to fitting in, emotions, bullies, school, peer pressure, failure, anger, and more. Graphic-novel-style illustrations engage even reluctant readers. Quotes from boys, survey results, facts, and stories keep them interested. Journaling prompts personalize the experience. For ages 9–13.
128 pp.; softcover; 2-color; illust.; 8" x 10½"

The Teen Guide to Global Action
How to Connect with Others (Near & Far) to Create Social Change
by Barbara A. Lewis

Kids everywhere are deciding they can't wait to become adults to change the world. They're acting right now to fight hunger and poverty, promote health and human rights, save the environment, and work for peace. Their stories prove that young people can make a difference on a global scale. This book includes real-life stories to inspire young readers, plus a rich menu of opportunities for service, fast facts, hands-on activities, user-friendly tools, and up-to-date resources kids can use to put their own volunteer spirit into practice. Upbeat, practical, and highly motivating, this book has the power to rouse young readers everywhere. For ages 12 & up.
144 pp.; softcover; 2-color; illust.; 7" x 9"

Be Fit, Be Strong, Be You
by Rebecca Kajander, C.P.N.P., M.P.H., and Timothy Culbert, M.D.

Tweens learn fun, empowering ways to take control of their fitness and diet and maintain healthy self-esteem. Whether they are underweight, overweight, or just the right weight, this book shows kids how to take a positive, holistic approach to their health and be the boss of their own wellness. Specific tips on eating, exercise, and self-esteem include planning meals and healthy "grabbable snacks," food journaling, getting daily exercise, using affirmations, and practicing complementary healthcare skills such as positive imagery and yoga. Kids learn how their body, mind, and spirit are connected and work together to make a whole, healthy self. Ages 8 & up.
96 pp.; softcover; color illust.; 6" x 8"

Middle School Confidential™ Series
by Annie Fox, M.Ed.

"Hey. We go to Milldale Middle School. We're very different in lots of ways, but we're all good friends." These timely and engaging survival guides for the middle school years follow Jack, Jen, Chris, Abby, Mateo, and Michelle as they try to figure out the social scene, forge friendships, deal with family dynamics, and navigate challenging situations. Featuring a blend of fiction and practical advice for the middle school years, the series provides the answers kids need in a contemporary, graphic-novel format that will draw in even reluctant readers. Filled with character narratives, quizzes, insider quotes from real kids, tips, tools, and resources, the books can be used in a variety of settings including homeroom, advisory time, counseling groups, and life skills classes. For ages 11–14.
Each book: *96 pp.; softcover; color illust.; 6" x 8"*

Be Confident in Who You Are Book 1
Real Friends vs. the Other Kind Book 2
What's Up with My Family? Book 3

What Do You Stand For? For Teens
A Guide to Building Character
by Barbara A. Lewis

This books invites teens to explore and practice honesty, kindness, integrity, tolerance, respect, and more. Includes inspiring quotations, thought-provoking dilemmas, activities, and stories about real kids who exemplify positive character traits. Resources point the way toward character-building books, organizations, programs, and websites. For ages 11 & up.
288 pp.; softcover; B&W photos & illust.; 8½" x 11"

Interested in purchasing multiple quantities? Contact edsales@freespirit.com or call 1.800.735.7323 and ask for Education Sales.

Many Free Spirit authors are available for speaking engagements, workshops, and keynotes. Contact speakers@freespirit.com or call 1.800.735.7323.

For pricing information, to place an order, or to request a free catalog, contact:

Free Spirit Publishing Inc.
217 Fifth Avenue North • Suite 200 • Minneapolis, MN 55401-1299
toll-free 800.735.7323 • local 612.338.2068 • fax 612.337.5050
help4kids@freespirit.com • www.freespirit.com